The
Power
of a
Positive
Team

The
Power
of a
Positive
Team

Proven Principles and
Practices That Make Great
Teams Great

JON GORDON

WILEY

Published by John Wiley & Sons, Inc., Hoboken, New Jersey.
Published simultaneously in Canada.

For general information on our other products and services or for technical
support, please contact our Customer Care Department within the United States at
(800) 762-2974, outside the United States at (317) 572-3993 or fax (317) 572-4002.

Wiley publishes in a variety of print and electronic formats and by print-on-demand.
Some material included with standard print versions of this book may not be included
in e-books or in print-on-demand. If this book refers to media such as a CD or DVD
that is not included in the version you purchased, you may download this material at
http://booksupport.wiley.com. For more information about Wiley products, visit
www.wiley.com.

Library of Congress Cataloging-in-Publication Data:

Names: Gordon, Jon, 1971– author.
Title: The power of a positive team : proven principles and practices that
    make great teams great / by Jon Gordon.
Description: Hoboken, New Jersey : John Wiley & Sons, Inc., [2018] | Includes
    bibliographical references. |
Identifiers: LCCN 2018007913 (print) | LCCN 2018010036 (ebook) | ISBN
    9781119430599 (epub) | ISBN 9781119430803 (pdf) | ISBN 9781119430247
    (cloth)
Subjects: LCSH: Teams in the workplace. | Organizational behavior. | Optimism.
Classification: LCC HD66 (ebook) | LCC HD66 .G6723 2018 (print) | DDC
    658.4/022–dc23
LC record available at https://lccn.loc.gov/2018007913

Printed in the United States of America

F10002731_073018

For my wife, Kathryn, and my children, Jade and Cole.
You are my team and I thank you for making me better.

Contents

Contents

Contents

No One Creates Success Alone

We are better together, and together we accomplish great things.

No one creates success alone. We all need a team to be successful. We are better together, and together we accomplish great things. Teams publish a book like this. Teams win Super Bowls and championships. Teams launch rockets into outer space. Teams perform open heart surgery and find cures for diseases. Teams design, build, and sell automobiles, phones, computers, video games, software, homes, and the latest and greatest products. Teams create commercials, movies, songs, and advertisements. Teams educate children in schools and run nonprofits that feed the poor, heal the sick, shelter the homeless, and provide safe drinking water in developing countries. Teams mobilize support for victims of natural disasters and help fight human trafficking. Teams work together to launch initiatives, companies, brands, products, and missions that change the world.

I know about teams. I've been on teams most of my life. My older brother played youth football and, at the age of six, I begged my parents to let me be on his team. I was too young to play, but they let me join in and gave me a jersey with the number ½ on it. Growing up I was a part of numerous youth sports teams, and in high school I played basketball, lacrosse, and football. In college I played on the Cornell lacrosse team and the experience had a profound impact on my life. As an adult I have been a part of restaurant teams as a waiter, bartender, and eventual owner. I served on a school team as a teacher and worked on a sales team as a salesperson for a technology company. I've been on several leadership teams for start-up businesses and nonprofits, and I even led a political campaign team when I ran for the Atlanta City Council at the age of 26.

Now I lead a team at work and I'm second-in-command of my team at home. I also get the opportunity to speak to and consult with numerous businesses, educational organizations, nonprofits, and professional and college sports teams. I didn't plan it, but I've become someone that leaders call when they need help developing high-performing and winning teams.

I've discovered over the years that a positive, united team is a powerful team. It doesn't happen by accident. A positive team is created by a group of individuals who come together with vision, purpose, passion, optimism, grit, excellence, communication, connection, love, care, and commitment to do something amazing and create something incredible together. I believe that everyone wants to be part of a great team, but not everyone knows how to become a great team.

That's why I wrote this book. I previously wrote *The Power of Positive Leadership* and *You Win in the Locker Room First*, but they were written to help leaders build their teams. I also wrote *The Hard Hat*, which is about how to be a great teammate, but that was meant more for the individual. This book is meant for teams to read together. I wrote it in such a way that team members could read it together and understand what they need to do to be a positive and connected team. In my work with teams, and through interviews with people who were part of some of the greatest teams in history, I've discovered proven principles and practices that make great teams great. I have shared these principles and practices in this book and my hope is that you will read them with your team, discuss what you need to do to be a great team, and then take action together. If you are willing to learn together, grow together, unite together, and act together, you will accomplish more than you ever thought possible.

Chapter 1

The Power of Positive

*Positivity is more than a state of mind.
It's a power that gives teams a competitive
advantage in business, sports, creativity, and life.*

I don't encourage teams to be positive just because it's more fun, enjoyable, and rewarding to be part of a positive team. I am passionate about creating positive teams because I know that positive teams are also more engaged and more likely to overcome all the forces against them and make a greater impact.

It's challenging to work toward a vision and create a positive future. It's difficult to launch new ideas, products, movies, missions, and organizations. It's not easy to pursue greatness and do what has never been done before. As a team you will face all kinds of adversity, negativity, and tests. There will be times when it seems as if everything in the world is conspiring against you and your team. There will be moments you want to give up. There will be days when your vision seems more like fantasy than reality. That's why becoming a positive team is so important. When I talk about positive teams, I am not talking about Pollyanna positivity, where you wear rose-colored glasses and ignore the reality of the situation. Positive teams are not about fake positivity. They are about real optimism, vision, purpose, and unity that make great teams great. Positive teams confront the reality of challenging situations and work together to overcome them.

Pessimistic teams don't become legendary. Negative teams talk about and create problems but they don't solve them. Throughout history we see that it's the positive teams that create the future and change the world. The future belongs to those who believe in it and work together with other positive people in order to create it.

I have witnessed the power of a positive team, and the research supports that positivity is a difference maker. Research by Manju Puri and David Robinson at Duke University found that optimistic people were more likely to succeed in business, sports, and politics. Relationship expert John Gottman's pioneering research found that marriages are much more likely to succeed when the couple experiences a five-to-one ratio of positive to negative interactions; when the ratio approaches a one-to-one ratio, marriages are more likely to end in divorce.

The positive energy you share with your team is significant. According to organizational expert Wayne Baker, who works with fellow researcher Robert Cross, "the more you energize people in your workplace, the higher your work performance." Baker says that this occurs because people want to be around you. You attract talent and people are more likely to devote discretionary time to your projects. They'll offer new ideas, information, and opportunities to you before others."

When you have a group of people doing this on a team, you create a positive feedback loop that makes your team operate at a higher level. Many think that you have to choose between positivity and winning, but you don't. Positivity leads to winning. The research is clear. Positivity is more than a state of mind. It's a power that gives teams a competitive advantage in business, sports, creativity, and life.

Since there are many different types of teams, I made it a point to include various examples from business, education, sports, music, technology, and more. Please know that even though I share a number of examples of sports teams, I'm aware that not everyone is a sports fan. However, I want to make it clear that the reason why I share these examples is to demonstrate how these principles work in real life.

The great thing about sports teams is that you can observe the effectiveness of these principles over the course of a season. You can tell who has become a positive team and who hasn't. You can see it in person and on television. I've been fortunate to work with many sports teams, and they are great case studies. And since I've also worked with countless businesses and schools, I can assure you the same principles apply to every team and organization. If you are not a fan of sports, simply take the sports example and think about how it applies to your team. You will discover a number of great ideas to make your team better.

Positive teams don't happen by accident. They happen when team members invest their time and energy to create a positive culture; work toward a shared vision with a greater purpose; work together with optimism and belief and overcome the negativity that too often sabotages teams and organizations. Positive teams take on the battle, overcome the negativity, face the adversity, and keep moving forward. They communicate, connect, commit, and encourage each other. They build relationships and trust that makes them stronger.

Positive teams commit to the mission and to each other. Instead of serving themselves, they serve one another. They care more about their effort, work, and teammates than they do about all the distractions vying for their attention. People on positive teams have a lot of belief in each other, a lot of love for each other, and a lot of desire to accomplish something great together. They pursue excellence and always strive to get better and make their team better. They lose their ego in the service of their team and find an uncommon collective greatness in the process. Because they care more, they do more, invest more, commit more, and accomplish more.

The Power of a Positive Team

Chapter 2

Positive Teams Create Positive Cultures

*Behind every great team is a strong culture; great
leadership; and passionate, committed people.*

There's a reason why all great teams have a great culture. It's because culture is the living and breathing essence of what a team believes, values, and does. Team culture is the written and unwritten rules that say how a team communicates, connects, thinks, works, and acts.

Culture isn't just one thing. It's everything. Culture drives expectations and beliefs. Expectations and beliefs drive behaviors. Behaviors drive habits. And habits create the future.

When Apple was just the two Steves (Jobs and Wozniak), they knew the culture they wanted to create. They would be the culture that challenged the status quo. Everything they did, including hiring people, running campaigns, and creating products, was influenced by this culture. Even now, the culture continues to influence everything they do and the way they do it. It's why Apple is famous for its maxim, "Culture beats strategy." You have to have the right strategy, of course, but it is your culture that will determine whether your strategy is successful.

Your most important job as a team is to create a culture—and not just any culture. You must create a positive culture that energizes and encourages each other, fosters connected relationships and great teamwork, empowers and enables your team to learn and grow, and provides an opportunity for you to do your best work.

Create Your Culture

When I was a sophomore on the Cornell lacrosse team we were ranked ninth in the country. I was the starting face-off midfielder and we played a tough game against West Point that went into sudden-death overtime, which means the first team to score wins. I remember standing at the face-off circle in the middle of the field thinking, *If I lose this face-off we will likely lose the game. I need to win it.*

I lost the face-off and, the next thing I knew, my opponent was running down the field along the sideline with the ball. I was so mad that I ran as fast as I could and somehow caught up and hit him really hard and the ball fell out of his stick. I picked it up before he did and, as he pushed me out of bounds, I jumped in the air and threw the ball behind my back to my friend and teammate, John Busse, who caught the ball with one hand and threw it to our other teammate, Joe Lando, who scored the game winner for us.

Please know I'm not telling you this to impress you with my athletic ability. It was my one and only great play in college. I'm telling you this because we won so many close games that year. But during my senior year, we lost a lot of close games. We even had a chance to beat Princeton, who won the national championship, in overtime but couldn't pull it off.

Looking back, I can see that the clear difference between my sophomore year and my senior year was our team culture. We had lost the championship culture that had been created. As Boston Celtics head coach Brad Stevens says, "Your culture is not just your tradition. It's the people in the locker room who carry it on." Unfortunately, my fellow teammates and I didn't create or carry on the culture of our older teammates before us.

I wish I had been the leader then that I am now but, unfortunately, I wasn't. I didn't know how important culture was to the success of a team. I didn't know you could lose your culture. I didn't know that culture and performance could change so quickly. I now know that building a great team begins with creating a great a culture. I know that, as a team, you are always creating your culture. You are creating culture every moment of every day by what you think, say, and do. It doesn't matter what your culture was like yesterday or last year. What matters is what you are doing to create it today.

Culture Is Dynamic, Not Static

People often look to leadership when it comes to the culture of an organization and team—and they should. Leaders have a huge influence on the culture. They set the tone and decide what the team values and stands for, but it's important to note that your culture is brought to life and created by everyone on your team.

You and your team members have a huge influence on your culture and the culture you create. It's not just about what your manager, school principal, boss, coach, or supervisor says and does. It's also about what you say and do. If you are a part of a negative culture, don't see yourself as a victim and by-product of it. Instead get together with your team and create a positive culture to replace it.

Culture is not static; it's dynamic. You can change it by what you say. You can elevate it by what you think. You can improve it by what you share. You can transform it by what you do. You can be a positive team that creates a positive culture right now.

Make Your Bus Great

People often ask me what to do if they are part of an organization with a negative culture but desire to have a positive culture in their department or team. I tell them what I shared in my book, *The Energy Bus*.

You may not be driving the big bus but you can make your own bus great. Create the culture of your team and show the rest of the organization what a positive team looks like.

Over the years I've had many teams do this and report to me that their team inspired other teams. In some cases, the positive team became the model for the entire organization, and transformed it as a result.

Never doubt the impact that a positive team can have on its organization, community, and, ultimately, the world. When you make your bus great, you show what's possible and help others drive toward greatness.

Make Your Culture a Priority

The University of Southern California (USC) men's tennis team won four national championships from 2009–2012. When I asked head coach Peter Smith what made these teams great, he didn't talk about talent. He talked about the culture they had created and the fact that Steve Johnson, arguably the greatest college tennis player of all time, bought into it as a team leader—and the team bought into Steve and the culture as well. They always had championship-quality players but for those four years, they had a championship culture too. It was a culture of love, accountability, family, and respect.

While USC was winning championships, Brian Boland and the University of Virginia (UVA) men's tennis team were coming close each year, but falling short. Brian Boland had been the UVA men's tennis coach since 2001 and, year after year, his teams were talented. They often made the quarters, semifinals, and even a few finals, but fell short of winning a championship. But in 2013 everything changed and they won four out of the next five national championships.

I asked Brian what happened and he said, "I changed. We changed. I was a hard driver and all about the outcome. I never said it but my guys knew it. In 2013 I made culture our focus and the team became culture and process focused instead of outcome focused. We worked to become a great team instead of just a bunch of individuals who wanted to win a championship."

I'll share some of the team-building process Brian took his team through later in the book, but the point is that an improvement in a team's culture changes everything for the better. In my work with businesses, schools, and hospitals, I have witnessed this often as well. Great things happen when a team makes culture their top priority.

Invest in the Root

I remember talking to Erik Spoelstra, the head coach of the Miami Heat, a few years ago. He told me that in past years, when the season ended, he focused 100 percent of his time on watching film and studying X's and O's. But now he spends most of his time on culture. I've spoken to his staff and team over the last few years, and you can tell they have a special culture. From the training staff to the coaching staff to the players and operations staff, they make their culture a top priority. They know it matters. They know it's important. They know they may not always have the best players, but they can always work to create the best culture. So can you.

You may not have the most talented team, but you can work to create the best team culture. There's a lot you can't control, but you can control how much time, energy, and care you invest in your culture.

I'm not going to lie and say that talent isn't important to be a successful team. No matter what kind of team you have, it helps to have talent. But culture drives your talent toward greatness. I've seen many teams with a lot of talent and a bad culture perform poorly. Too many teams focus on the fruit of the tree. They focus on the outcome, the numbers, the stock price, the test scores, the profit, and the wins and losses. They focus on the fruit and ignore the root (their culture, people, relationships, and process). They think it's the numbers that matter most.

What they don't realize is that it's not the numbers that drive the culture and process; it's the culture and process that drive the numbers. The fruit is just a by-product of how well you invest in the root. If you focus on the fruit and ignore the root, the tree will die. If you invest in the root and make culture a priority, you will receive an abundant and steady supply of fruit. I want to encourage you to be a team that invests in the root.

Decide to Be Vitamin C

You are contagious. The energy you put into your team and culture determines the quality of it.

Research from the Heart Math Institute (HeartMath.org) shows that when you have a feeling in your heart, it goes to every cell in the body, then outward—and people up to 10 feet away can sense these feelings. This means that each day you are broadcasting to your team how you feel. You are broadcasting negative energy or positive energy, apathy or passion, indifference or purpose. Research from Harvard University also supports the idea that the emotions you feel are contagious and affect the people around you.

Your team is just as likely to catch your bad mood as the flu, and on the flip side, they will catch your good mood as well. As a team member, your attitude, energy, and leadership are contagious, and has a big impact on your culture and team. When you walk into the office, or the meeting, or into the school, hospital, or locker room, you have a decision to make. Are you going to be a germ to your team or a big dose of Vitamin C?

Please know that you don't have to be an extrovert to be positively contagious. Sharing positive energy doesn't mean you have to be a rah-rah person and bounce off the walls. It means that, from the heart, you simply broadcast the love, passion, positivity, and purpose that you have for your team. It means that you decide to be a fountain of energy instead of an energy drain. It means that you infuse your team with positive energy instead of being an energy vampire that sucks the life out of them.

Great teams are collectively positive and positively contagious. They give and share positive energy to each other, and the more they give, the more comes back to them.

The Power Is on the Inside

It's your culture and your team. Own it. Don't expect someone else to create it. You and your team have the power to create a positive culture. A positive team that creates a positive culture is well on their way to achieving positive results. Of course there's more to the story and that involves the principles and practices to help you create a strong culture, which I will share in the rest of the book.

As you create your culture it's important to know that there will be forces from the outside that seek to sabotage it. There will also be negativity on the inside that can negatively impact it. As you read the rest of the book, keep in mind that the stronger you are on the inside, the more you can withstand the outside forces. You really do win in the locker room before you win on the field. You win in the teachers' lounge before you win the hearts and minds of your students. You win in the office before you win in the marketplace. The power is on the inside.

What Do We Want to Be?

Considering all I've said about creating your culture, I want to close with probably the most important key to help you create it. To create your culture you must identify what you stand for and what you want to be known for.

I had the opportunity to speak to Southwest Airlines a few years ago. They told me how consultants suggested they charge passengers to check luggage since the competition was doing it and Southwest could make a lot more money with this additional source of revenue. Southwest considered their proposal, but in the process asked themselves an important question: Is this what we stand for? They went straight to their purpose statement: "To connect people to what's important in their lives through friendly, reliable, and low-cost air travel." They ultimately decided that if they were focused on everyday fliers and low-cost air travel, they shouldn't charge baggage fees.

You might think they missed out on a lot of money because of their decision, but a funny thing happened. Southwest started to get new customers because the airline didn't charge for checked bags. They ran advertising campaigns highlighting the fact that bags fly free, and they gained market share in the process. Their revenue grew to new heights. It's a great example to illustrate that once you know what you stand for, decisions are easy to make. When your culture dictates your decisions, you are on the right path to positive results.

I recently gave a talk to the leaders of a major pharmaceutical company. I asked them what made their team great. One manager raised his hand and said that he and his team took some time together in a meeting room and asked themselves "What do we want to be?" They asked what kind of culture they wanted to create. What kind of team did they want to be? What did they want to accomplish together? He said his title may have been "leader," but he felt like his team was leading him in the discussion. The

23

Positive Teams Create Positive Cultures

conversation was incredible and they decided together what they wanted to be.

Since then they have become an incredibly high-performing team. The manager said he feels more like a team member than a leader because the team members lead each other. They know what they stand for, they know what kind of team they want to be, and their culture dictates their direction and decisions.

You can do the same with your team. Identify what you stand for. What do you want to be known for? What kind of team do you want to be? When you know what you want to be, you can create your culture to become it.

Chapter 3

Positive Teams Work Together toward a Shared Vision with a Greater Purpose

When you know your why and you know the way,
you won't let obstacles get in the way.

When Alan Mulally became the CEO of Ford in 2006, he brought a wealth of experience from his role turning around the airplane manufacturer, Boeing. He also brought the knowledge that in order to turn around the automaker, which just had a loss of $12 billion, he would have to unite the company around a shared vision and purpose.

As I wrote about in *The Power of Positive Leadership*, Alan created a One Ford culture to unite everyone in the company, to bring them together as one team with one purpose, working on one plan to achieve one goal. Alan told me that everyone had to know the plan, embrace the plan, and relentlessly work toward the plan. Alan and his One Ford team succeeded, and many say it was one of the greatest leadership feats in history.

I believe one of the big reasons why was because Alan had rallied Ford around a shared vision and a greater purpose. I have found that your team success starts with having a shared vision of where your team is going, and a greater purpose of why you are going there.

When you know your why and you know the way, you won't let obstacles get in the way. You will keep moving forward toward the shared vision you have, and your greater purpose will fuel you on the journey.

Shared Vision

The key words here are "shared vision." It's a vision that the entire team shares. It's one vision that unites and inspires the team members individually and collectively. This one vision serves as a North Star that moves everyone on the team in the same direction.

As a team, you must continually point each other toward this North Star. Yes, we were *here* yesterday, but *this* is where we are going. Yes, we faced this challenge, but here's where we are going now. We don't have a perfect set of plans because the world is always changing, but we do have a vision and a North Star that will guide us. We don't have a perfect road map, but we have a path forward and we have each other. Together we can reach our vision if we keep our eyes on the North Star and move toward it together.

Greater Purpose

The other key words are "greater purpose." Research shows people are most energized when they are using their strengths for a bigger purpose, one that goes beyond themselves as individuals.

It's a purpose beyond oneself that truly drives and energizes people and teams. It's not just about having a shared vision. It's also having a greater purpose that drives you toward your shared vision.

It's essential for you and your team to understand why you exist and the difference your team can make. When each member of the team knows their team's purpose and how they can contribute to it, the collective energy and passion will soar. For example, my friend John Rauvola, the president of Superfeet, knew that over 75 percent of the US adult population has foot pain, so he and his team created a bigger purpose: "To make a positive difference in people's lives by establishing a strong foundation." HP recently selected Superfeet to introduce the first foot scanning and pressure plate analysis, which results in 3D-printed custom insoles and custom footwear produced at the Superfeet manufacturing facility. One of the main reasons why they were selected was because the Superfeet team was driven by purpose and was said to have amazing positive energy regarding this project.

Purpose-Driven Goals

One of the most powerful ways to be a powerful team is to have purpose-driven goals rather than numerical goals.

For example, for years I chose Organic Valley milk over other brands in the supermarket. I had no idea why it appealed to me until I spoke at their remote headquarters surrounded by acres of farmland in the middle of Wisconsin. I discovered a company that didn't believe in sales and revenue goals. Of course they forecasted sales for budgetary, planning, and growth purposes, and they measured numbers and outcomes, but they did so with the belief that numbers were just a by-product of how well they were living and sharing their purpose.

Instead of focusing on numerical goals, Organic Valley passionately focused on their purpose-driven goals: providing opportunities for farmers to make a living, sustainability of the land, and providing families with healthy dairy products that were free of hormones and antibiotics. The result: Organic Valley's numbers kept growing and growing.

While speaking to an NFL team a few years ago, I had each player write their goals on a piece of paper. After a few minutes, I had them rip up the paper they had just written on.

You could hear the complaints and feel their anger and frustration while they ripped up the paper they had just spent time and energy writing on. I then asked, "How many of you wrote down win a Super Bowl, win x number of games, achieve x number of yards, have x number of interceptions, and so on?" All the hands went up.

I told them that every person in every NFL meeting room has the same goals. It's not the goals that will make you successful, otherwise everyone and every team would be successful after writing down their goals. Instead, it's your commitment to the process, your growth and your purpose that drives you to reach these goals, that will determine what you accomplish. I then had them write down their commitments and purpose for playing and had them share with the rest of the team. It was powerful.

The truth is that numbers and goals don't drive people. People with a purpose drive the numbers and achieve goals.

Now this doesn't mean you shouldn't measure numbers or have goals. You need to measure the numbers. In many cases, you need to have revenue targets and similar metrics. Numbers are to your purpose what a scale and measuring tape are to a diet. It's an indicator of how you are doing. Every organization wants to beat last year's numbers. Every nonprofit wants to help more people. Every school wants to empower more children. Every hospital wants to reduce patient deaths and save more lives.

It's great to have a goal you want to achieve, but once you identify a goal or outcome, you will be more powerful and energized if you are tapping into a bigger purpose in order to reach your numbers and goals. Your greater purpose will lead to greater performance!

Vision + Mission

People often ask me if a vision and mission should be separate or combined into one statement. I know many teams and organizations have separate vision and mission statements. I think that's perfectly fine, but I like to combine a vision and mission statement together. I believe every team member should be able to look at their North Star and say, *this is where we are going and this is why we are going there. This is what we are creating together and this is why we are creating it.*

Whether you can do that in one statement or two doesn't matter. What matters is that you have a team with a vision that's on a mission. Make the time to create your vision and mission statement together and then make even more time to live it. After all, you can have the greatest vision and mission statements in the world, but it's pointless if you don't have people who are on a mission.

Almost every organization has a mission statement today, but only the great ones have people who are on a mission. Unfortunately, too many teams get burned out because they forget their purpose. We don't get burned out because of what we do. We get burned out because we forget why we do it. Remember your why and you won't lose your energy along the way.

Telescope and Microscope

As a team you will want to carry a metaphorical telescope and microscope with you on your journey. The telescope helps you and your team keep your eyes on the vision and North Star to remind you of the big picture and your greater purpose. The microscope helps you zoom in to focus on the things you must do in the short term to realize the vision in your telescope.

If you have only a telescope, then you'll be thinking about your vision all the time and dreaming about the future, but not taking necessary steps to realize it. If you have only a microscope, then you'll be working hard every day, but setbacks and challenges will likely frustrate and discourage you because you'll lose sight of the big picture and forget your purpose.

You need to frequently pull out your telescope to remind yourself and your team where you are going and why you are going there, and you'll need to look through the microscope daily in order to focus on what matters most and follow through on your commitments. Together they will help take your team where you want to go and keep you energized for the journey.

Creating *Billions* and Winning Gold

When Brian Koppelman and his writing partner David Levien looked into their metaphorical telescope they saw billions. Not billions of stars, but rather the megahit television show *Billions*. The duo that created movie hits such *Ocean's Thirteen* and *Rounders* have worked together for years with a shared vision and a greater purpose to become one of Hollywood's most successful writing teams.

When I asked Brian their secret, he said that he and David were always mission focused and purpose driven. He said, whatever movie, show, or project they were working on, they knew that the work they were creating was the important thing and their job was to work together to serve the purpose of making it the best it could be. They believed that if they focused on making something great, that would allow them to tell more stories together. The movie or show was the vision they were working toward, and the purpose was to make it great.

Their commitment was to the project and to each other. Egos didn't surface because everything they did together was to serve their vision and mission. I've learned from them that egos don't get in the way when you have a team that is driven by a shared vision and a greater purpose. A team with a vision on a mission doesn't let division stop them.

Whether it's creating *Billions* or winning Olympic gold medals, the same principles apply. The same day I spoke to Brian Koppelman I also spoke to Kerri Walsh Jennings. Kerri and Misty May-Treanor make up the greatest beach volleyball team of all time. Together they won gold medals at the 2004, 2008, and 2012 Olympics, and they also won the FIVB Beach Volleyball World Championship three times.

When I asked Kerri what made her and Misty a great team she said, "We knew where we wanted to go. We had a vision and a goal, and were comfortable about what we had to do to get there. We wanted to be truly great. We owned our deep desire to kick ass. We had a lot of love for the game and each other. We were excited about doing this together. From the

33

beginning, we were committed to each other and our mission. We knew what we had to do together, and it was about achieving greatness together."

I had to smile. I spoke to Kerri only a few hours after I spoke to Brian and their answers were amazingly similar. I realized in that moment that a team with talent can be good, but they must have a shared vision and a greater purpose in order to be great.

The World's Largest Family

I'm not sure you'll find a bigger purpose than rescuing orphans and making them a part of your family. But that's what Charles Mully and his wife, Esther, have been doing since 1989.

Charles Mully was abandoned by his family at the age of 6 and forced to live and beg on the streets of Kenya for most of his childhood. At 17, he walked 70 kilometers to Nairobi, where he worked several jobs before becoming an entrepreneur and starting his own transportation company at the age of 23. Over the next two decades Mully transformed his one-vehicle operation into an agricultural, oil, and gas business conglomerate that made him a very wealthy man. Mully had it all—a happy marriage, seven children, and all the advantages of wealth and success.

One day he encountered a group of kids who lived on the streets like he did as a child, and he couldn't get them out of his mind. He knew he had to do something and that something turned into the unthinkable. Mully and Esther sold everything they owned and spent their fortune to rescue, house, nurture, educate, and help kids from the streets of Kenya. They gave up everything to help those who had nothing.

Mully Children's Family (MCF) has since transformed the lives of thousands of street kids. It is estimated that since 1989 Mully and his wife have taken in 13,000 abandoned children and made them part of their family. Many of them have since attended college and become successful teachers, doctors, nurses, business professionals, and entrepreneurs. Other children have returned to MCF as adults to transform the lives of the next generation of Mully's children.

In reading this I hope you don't gloss over the numbers. Let them really sink in. We are talking about *13,000 children*! Thirteen thousand children with no home, no family, no future! But one selfless, positive team (Charles and Esther) gave up their fortune and comfortable life to change the world, one child at a time. And the number continues to grow—there are currently 3,000 children housed by MCF.

Mully is known as the father of the fatherless and the father to the world's biggest family. There was a movie about him that impacted my family and me greatly. Watch it with your family and team to see what happens when a team has a shared vision and greater purpose. It will make you a better team. When you have a shared vision and greater purpose, you can make miracles happen.

The Table

I don't have a family of 13,000 people but I did want to unite my family of four around a shared vision and greater purpose. At the advice of my friend Dan Britton, we started having a family meeting each Sunday. We came up with a family vision and mission together, and each week we sat around the kitchen

Positive Teams Work Together toward a Shared Vision

table and talked about how we were doing living the vision and mission. We talked about the challenges we were facing and possible solutions going forward. My kids played sports, I traveled a lot, and our world was often busy and chaotic, but making time to sit around the table and talk each week was a key part for us in building a strong family team.

I know you and your team are busy as well. You have so much to do and only so many hours in the day to do it. But make sure you take time for what matters most. Make time to create and revisit your vision and mission so that you can make them come alive.

Keep Your Vision and Purpose Alive

I find that a lot of teams start out with a vision and purpose but, as the year progresses and they face adversity and challenges, they often lose their vision.

I want to encourage you to write down your vision and purpose and find ways to keep them alive. If you don't keep them alive they will fade away. You have to be intentional as a team. Talk about the vision and purpose often. Envision the future together. Create tangible reminders and pictures.

The Cornell University lacrosse team carries a red hard hat with them. I remember watching their game on television years ago and never saw a team play with such passion and purpose. I had to find out what drove this team to play this way. I met with the coach, Jeff Tambroni, and he told me about the hard hat. It was given to the freshman on the team who was the hardest worker, the most loyal, and most selfless player. He told me about George Boiardi, who carried the hard hat as a freshman. George died on the field his senior year after jumping in front of a shot and getting hit in the chest with the ball. Jeff told me how the hard hat came to symbolize more than just being a selfless player with a blue-collar work ethic. It came to symbolize George and the kind of teammate he was. Jeff told me how the team decided to play the rest of the season to honor George and be the kind of teammate he was. He told me how he brought the hard hat on the field, and anytime the team was not giving their best effort, he would use it to remind them of their purpose.

When I watched this team play, I saw a team that had a shared vision and a bigger purpose. The hard hat was a tangible reminder of their purpose to play to honor George. They were playing for more than themselves. They were playing for him.

Make Your Vision and Purpose Come Alive

In addition to keeping your vision and purpose alive, you want to make your vision and purpose come alive. This means that each person on your team lives the vision and mission. They see it with their own eyes and are inspired from their own heart. For the vision and purpose to come alive, it must have meaning for each team member.

For example, before I spoke to a leadership team at Palmetto Health in South Carolina, I interviewed a bunch of people who worked in the organization's hospitals and asked them about the Palmetto vision and what it meant to them. Amazingly, each person was able to recite the vision and mission and tell me specifically what it meant to them and how it inspired them.

It's powerful to have each team member identify and share what the vision and mission means to them and how they can contribute to it. The research shows that when people know how they are contributing to a shared vision and a bigger purpose, engagement and passion soars. A shared vision and greater purpose is brought to life one person, one team at a time.

One Word

One of the most powerful ways I have found to help teams live their vision and mission is through One Word. Each year, each member of the team picks a word that will inspire them to live with more meaning and mission, passion, and purpose for that year.

My friends Dan Britton and Jimmy Page have been doing this for over 20 years, and the words they choose each year have shaped and inspired their lives in many ways. About eight years ago, they told me how each year they, along with their family members, pick a word and, on New Year's Eve, each member of their family makes a painting of their word. They put the paintings in the kitchen as a reminder to live their word.

I thought it was really powerful and started doing it as well with my family, and then shared the idea with the various leaders and teams I worked with. It was catalytic and life changing. Leaders shared words like "love" and "dream" and "invest" and "go" and "execute" and "fearless" and "life" and "relationships." Dabo Swinney, the head coach of the Clemson football team, even said in an interview immediately after winning the National Championship, "My word all year was love, and I told my team that their love for each other was going to make the difference."

It's an idea that has taken off, and now thousands of teams pick a word each year to inspire them at work and home. Hendrick Auto, a major automotive retailer, even created a One-Word car to display in their headquarters. It is decorated with all the words of all their employees. When employees walk into the building they see their words and are reminded to live them. Schools have made One-Word T-shirts and create One-Word walls, and businesses and hospitals post their words in meeting rooms and offices.

When speaking about this idea, I ask people to pick a word but also to identify why they chose it. It's the *why* behind the word that gives it meaning and makes it a powerful purpose producer.

Make Sure Everyone Is on the Bus

When I think of a team, I envision them on a bus together moving toward their destination with a shared vision and greater purpose. If a team isn't on the bus together, then you know they aren't moving powerfully in the same direction.

It's essential that a team pauses along the way and makes sure that everyone is on the bus. You can't assume that just because you had a meeting about vision and purpose six months ago, everyone is still on the bus and excited about the journey. Don't think that just because you are on the same team or working in the same building, everyone is on the bus.

It's important to stop and ask, "Are we all on the bus?" If some team members are not on the bus, then you can discuss why and address the situation, as we will discuss later in the book.

Everyone Means *Everyone*

When I say *everyone*, I'm referring to more people than just the people on your team. *Everyone* includes the people who directly influence the people on your team.

For example, if you are a high school or college sports team, I highly recommend that the parents of the athletes also get on the bus. Parents can greatly influence the culture of their team through the beliefs and words they share with their children. Getting parents to understand and buy into the vision and purpose is a great way to make the culture and team stronger.

The same goes for businesses as well. When John Rauvola, the CEO of Superfeet, hosts off-site retreats with his leadership team, he also invites their spouses and significant others. He wants *everyone*, his leaders and their partners, to know about the organization's strategic initiatives and results. By understanding the challenges they are facing and their vision, purpose, and goals, the spouses and significant others feel a part of the team. This makes them more supportive and helps them understand how much energy and effort their husbands and wives need to invest to make the company successful. One spouse even said to her husband, "You need to go into work on Saturday. We need to make sure we reach that goal."

When *everyone* who influences the team gets on the bus together with a shared vision and greater purpose, the team becomes an unstoppable force of momentum and positive energy.

Chapter 4

Positive Teams Work Together with Optimism, Positivity, and Belief

A team that believes together achieves together.

As your team works toward a shared vision with a greater purpose, you will face all sorts of challenges and adversity. There will be days you want to give up. There will be times your obstacles seem insurmountable. There will be moments when it seems like your competition has you beat. Too often, I see teams give up because of the struggle, the circumstance, the frustration, the fear, the negativity, the rejection, and the adversity. They give up because the obstacle seems more powerful than them and they don't have the faith to keep moving forward. But you don't have to give up. You don't have to let fear win. You can know that all things are possible to a team that believes. You can trust that your obstacles are no match for a team that has faith, love, and hope. You can keep your shared vision and purpose alive and work with optimism, positivity, and belief to create it.

Stay Positive Together

A lot of teams start out positive. At the beginning of the season, project, campaign, or initiative, everyone is fired up and ready to go. But as time goes on and challenges emerge, the team loses its positive attitude and energy. I've found that great teams are not only positive in the beginning but throughout the journey. They stay positive together through all the adversity, challenges, setbacks, and issues.

I tell sports teams all the time that of course you are positive now during training camp. After all, you're undefeated. You haven't played a game yet, so you haven't lost a game. The key to your season will be if you stay positive together through the losses and throughout the year. A team that stays positive together succeeds together.

It works the same with schools. I was recently talking to Windy Hodge, a principal who has adopted our Energy Bus for Schools program. She told me that before they adopted our program, they were a school that focused on what was going wrong and what the students were doing wrong. But now her team of teachers is focused on what is going right. This positive approach has made an impact. While many teachers and school environments become increasingly negative throughout the school year, Windy and her team have stayed positive and made a greater difference as a result.

It sounds cliché, but so often the key to making your vision a reality is to just stay positive. Many teams don't and they sabotage themselves. But the teams that simply stay positive, one day at a time, end up accomplishing a lot over time.

Believe Together

When Dabo Swinney became the head coach of the Clemson University football team, he brought two signs with him to his first meeting with the team. One sign said, "I can't" with the "t" crossed out, and the other sign said "Believe." He knew there wasn't a lot of belief—either inside or outside the program—

that they could be great. Clemson was known for losing games they should win. It happened to them so often it became its own word: *Clemsoning.*

So the man who had never been a head coach or coordinator, whose father left when he was young, who was homeless for a time growing up, who had believed in himself enough to become a walk-on at Alabama, who had left coaching for a few years to pursue a career in real estate, and who had come to believe that anything was possible, knew his number-one priority was to inspire his team to believe—and he did.

Clemson is a team that is built on positive belief. Having worked with them for the past six years, I've witnessed how Dabo's belief has transferred to his team and, more importantly, I've seen how the players have transferred this belief to each other.

I was on the sidelines for the 2016–17 national championship when Alabama scored to take the lead with two minutes left in the game. It looked like Alabama was going to win, but Clemson quarterback Deshaun Watson gathered his offense together and said, "Let's be legendary. Let's be great." He and his team believed they were going to march down the field and win the game—and that's what they did. It was as if all the years and all the hard work and all the belief in themselves and each other came together in one final magical drive that saw them score a touchdown with four seconds left on the clock to win the national championship.

In *The Power of Positive Leadership*, I wrote about Dabo Swinney's belief and the impact it had on his team. It's also important to understand the belief that team members like Deshaun Watson had in their teammates.

45

The greatest teams don't just have great coaches, great managers, great principals, or great leaders at the helm. They have great leaders within the team who inspire their team to believe in each other.

It's powerful when you believe in your leader, but to be a great team I believe it's even more powerful to believe in each other. If you want to accomplish great things together, you must believe together.

Encourage Each Other

I'm a walker not a runner, but a few years ago I decided to join my friends Dan Britton, my *One Word* coauthor, and Chris Regan, a musician, for a five-mile run through the battlefields of Gettysburg, where I was spending time at an FCA lacrosse camp with my daughter.

It seemed like a good idea in theory, but after the second mile I wasn't feeling very positive about my decision. At the three-mile mark I wanted to stop running but knew it wasn't an option. As we ran the last two miles, mostly uphill, I felt like I was going to pass out, but with Dan and Chris's amazing encouragement, I kept going and somehow made it to the finish line. It was an incredible feeling.

The next day as I took a very slow walk to get the lactic acid out of my aching body I realized that there's no way I would have been able to run five miles by myself. I would have given up around the third mile if I had been on my own, but because I was with friends, I kept running. Because they encouraged me, I was able to power through the most difficult part of the run.

It's the same with you and your team. No one creates success alone. We all need a positive team to push and encourage us. We all need encouragement from our team.

As a team, make sure you encourage each other. Cheer each other on. Support each other. When you encourage each other, you make one another stronger and you make the team stronger.

Feed the Positive Dog

Great teams are collectively positive. They have a collective belief and contagious optimism—and a team's belief is made up of the belief of each individual. Each individual contributes to the collective optimism, belief, and positivity of a team. The fact is, if you don't have it, you can't share it. To be a positive team, all of your team members must cultivate optimism within themselves and share it with each other.

In my book *The Positive Dog*, Matt and Bubba are two dogs living in a shelter. Matt, who everyone calls Mutt, is really negative. Bubba is a positive dog, who teaches Matt an important lesson. He says that we all have two dogs inside of us, "We have a negative dog and a positive dog, and they fight all the time, but the one who wins the fight is the one you feed the most, so feed the positive dog."

I based this story on an ancient fable about two wolves, but whether we are talking about wolves, dogs, or humans, we all have a positive-versus-negative battle going on each day. Every moment and every situation presents an opportunity to your team to see and experience the positive or the negative. Each day, you can feed the positive dog or the negative dog inside yourselves, and whichever one you feed, grows.

As a team, you want to feed the positive dog. Feed yourselves. Feed each other. The more you feed the positive dog the more it grows, and the more the negative dog becomes smaller and weaker.

Talk to Yourself

When I think of feeding the positive dog, I think of Dr. James Gills, who accomplished the remarkable feat of completing a double triathlon (two triathlons back to back with only a 24-hour break) six times, and the last time he did it he was 59 years old.

When asked how he did it, he gave the best advice I've ever heard. He said, "I've learned to talk to myself instead of listen to myself." He memorized scripture and would recite it to himself when he needed a boost. Gills continued, "If I listen to myself, I hear all the reasons why I should give up. I hear that I'm too tired, too old, too weak to make it. But if I talk to myself, I can give myself the encouragement and words I need to hear to keep running and finish the race."

It's the same way with life. Too often we listen to ourselves and hear all the complaints, self-doubt, fear, and negativity that lead to unhappiness, failure, and unfulfilled goals. But just because you have a negative thought doesn't mean you have to believe it.

Many of your negative thoughts come from fear, and the truth is that fear is a liar. I've learned that instead of listening to the negative lies, we can choose to feed ourselves with the positive truth. We can speak truth to the lies and fuel up with words, thoughts, phrases, and beliefs that give us the strength and power to overcome our challenges and create an extra-ordinary life and team.

Whatever comes your way, just keep running, stay positive, talk to yourself (instead of listening to yourself), and make sure you celebrate and raise your hands in the air when you and your team have reached your destination!

Replace *Have To* with *Get To*

A lot of times, as individuals and teams, we stop appreciating the opportunity we have to do the work we do and the people we do it with. For some, work becomes an obligation. For others entitlement sets in and they stop appreciating the opportunity and journey.

A simple shift of a few words has the power to change the way you and your team approach everything. Instead of talking about what you *have to* do, start acknowledging what you *get to* do.

You get the opportunity to live this life. You get to work with a team that is making a difference. You get to learn and grow each day. You get to go to work, while so many others wish they had a job. You even get to drive in traffic, whereas many people can't afford to buy a car. You get to wake up, while so many others have passed on too early.

When you replace *have to* with *get to*, you change a complaining voice to an appreciative heart. And when you appreciate, you elevate yourself and your team.

Remember, life and work is a gift, not an obligation. Stop being entitled. Start appreciating all the opportunities you and your team have been given.

Make the Next Opportunity Great

Another way we feed the positive dog is through our perspectives and how we see the world.

While visiting with and speaking to several major league baseball teams during spring training, I kept hearing from players and coaches that baseball is "a game of failure." After all, even a Hall of Fame player will fail to get a hit two out of three times. And most players will fail to get a hit three out of four times. A pitcher will give up hits and home runs; fielders will make errors.

Yes, baseball is a game where people fail often. But I saw it differently and, when talking to the teams, I offered a different perspective. I said, "I don't believe baseball is a game of failure. I believe it's a game of opportunity! No matter what happened on the last play, pitch, or at bat, you get the opportunity to make the next one great."

It's the same way with life. Anyone pursuing anything worthwhile will fail and fail often. I've been on many teams that have failed, but in looking back, I realize we weren't failing; we were growing. We weren't failing; we were becoming. I've learned that you can dwell on the past or look forward to making the next opportunity great.

L.O.S.S.

Speaking of opportunity, it's essential as a team to see your challenges not as challenges but as opportunities. You will have failures. You will lose games, clients, projects, and people. But you don't have to let the *loss* bring you down. Instead, you can see it as a learning opportunity and stay strong. L.O.S.S. stands for "Learning Opportunity Stay Strong."

There was a British study of 500 fortunate people who seemed to have it all—wealth, relationships, great careers, and happiness. When the researchers studied these charmed people, they were surprised to find that every one of them had experienced misfortune in their lives. On the outside, it seemed like they had lived perfect lives, but every one of them had faced challenges, adversity, and hardships. Yet despite the various challenges, they all shared the same characteristic: They all turned their misfortune into fortune. In the midst of their struggle, they looked for and found an opportunity.

As a team, you must remember that events are going to happen. Challenges are going to come your way. Your job is to not get stuck in the mud. Don't sink to a lower level. Keep your head up. Look for the opportunity and the good that is coming your way. Ask, "How can we learn from this? How can we grow from this? What do we want to do now? What actions will we take?" Stay strong together and you will turn your challenges into even greater opportunities and results.

My friend Dwight Cooper, who is now the CEO of Talent Management Group, told me that during the great recession, when he was the CEO of PPR, they lost a lot of their business. But instead of wallowing and allowing the loss to get them down, they came together and asked themselves what opportunity presented itself to them. As a result, they saw a need for other human capital solutions in their business, founded three new divisions, and they quickly shifted their focus and attention to grow those parts of the business, which led to greater success and profits.

Shark or Goldfish

In *The Shark and the Goldfish*, I share how the waves of change are always coming your way, and when the wave hits, you have a choice as a team. You can resist change or you can ride the wave to a successful future.

The research shows that people, companies, and teams that thrived during the great recession were the ones that embraced the change. Instead of being like goldfish and waiting to be fed like in the good ole days, they embraced the change and looked for opportunities to find more food. The key factor in their success was their perspective, how they saw the change they were experiencing. Those who saw it as a bad thing and resisted it got crushed by the wave. Those who saw it as a good thing and an opportunity rode the wave to a better future.

Think Like Rookies

Too many teams have been infected by what I call the curse of experience. This is where they long for the good ole days, complain about the way things are, and are unwilling to change. They have allowed their past experience, good or bad, to affect their present and future.

I saw this a lot in real estate companies when I was brought in to boost morale during the great recession. Before my talk, companies often gave out awards to the best producers, and I realized that a lot of rookies were winning the awards. It hit me that many of the veterans, despite all their great experience, were so shaken up by the economy that they had become goldfish instead of sharks. They had allowed fear to paralyze them and circumstances to define them. They were complaining about the economy instead of creating it. They had the curse of experience, and the antidote was to get them to think like rookies again.

Rookies aren't tainted by rejection, negative assumptions, or past experiences. They bring an idealism, optimism, and passion to their work. They don't focus on what everyone says is impossible. Instead, with wide eyes, they believe anything is possible. Rookies put their heads down, work hard, stay positive, live fearlessly, and are naïve enough to be successful. Rookies don't have experience; they don't know about the way things were. They have no knowledge of the good ole days. Instead, rookies create their good ole days right now.

Regardless of how much experience you and your team have, I want to encourage you to let your experience be a blessing, not a curse. Let your experience provide you with expertise and let your rookie mind-set fuel you with optimism and passion. Think like a rookie, forget the past, and create your good ole days right now.

Defeat Murphy

I'm sure you have heard of Murphy's Law, right? Whatever can go wrong will go wrong—and usually at the worst possible time. Unfortunately, Murphy's Law seems to play out all too often and, when a series of bad things happens, it can lead you to expect more bad things to happen. Instead of hoping for the best, you start to expect the worst and act accordingly.

NFL Football coach Gus Bradley, one of the most positive leaders I've ever met, told me about a great way he helps his team deal with negative events (e.g., a crucial interception, penalty, injury, bad weather, etc.) and avoid the victim mindset that can accompany them. Gus tells his team about this fictional guy named Murphy whom the law is named after. Murphy is a big jerk who wants to ruin your practice, games, and season. He says that Murphy shows up at the worst possible time, but instead of being scared of him, they are going to tackle him. They expect to see Murphy and when they do, they have an even greater expectation that they will defeat him.

Life is filled with challenging circumstances, but you can rise above them. Life is hard, but you are strong. The struggle is real, but so is your ability to overcome it. As my friend Erwin McManus said, "Greatness is never born from easy circumstances. We can become stronger when the world becomes harder."

So when adversity hits, don't run from it. Don't be scared of it. Face it. Take it on and keep moving forward. Murphy is tough, but you are tougher.

Inside Out

A big part of the power of a positive team is knowing that you don't create the world outside in; you create it inside out. This means that your circumstances and the events that happen in the world are not meant to define you. You are meant to define your circumstances. The power is not in the circumstance, but rather in your state of mind and the love, passion, soul, purpose, and perspective that you create with.

Let's take traffic, for example. One day traffic really bothers you. Another day you are listening to a great song or podcast, you're in a great mood, and the traffic doesn't bother you. Is it the circumstance or your state of mind that produces how you feel? If it was the circumstance, your response to traffic would be the same, 100 percent of the time.

Remember that it's never about the circumstance. It's not the challenge, change, economy, adversity, or setback you and your team are facing. It's always your state of mind and your thinking that produces how you feel and respond.

Your company might be facing challenges, but you and your team can work positively and powerfully together and be a catalyst for the other departments. Your industry might be going through change and turmoil, but your team can change the industry by what you do together. Your school district might be dealing with budget cuts and change, but you can be a model school for everyone else to follow.

Don't look at the problems in the world and allow them to get you down. Look inside yourself and look at your team and decide to change the world inside out. Decide to show the world what a positive team looks like and what can be accomplished when a team works inside out. The power is on the inside, and when you and your team know this and live by it, you will create amazing and positive changes on the outside.

Distort Reality

As a positive team you really do have the power to distort reality. We often think that reality is objective, but when you understand how positive teams have changed the world throughout history, it becomes clear that a team can define reality and distort it in a positive way.

Before there was an iPhone, iPad, iCloud, or Apple Watch, there was Steve Jobs, a man with vision, positive ideas, and a reality-distortion field. In Walter Isaacson's biography *Steve Jobs*, Isaacson describes how Jobs repeatedly convinced Apple employees that they could meet project deadlines that everyone thought was impossible. Time and time again they would tell Steve he was being unrealistic and there was no way they could create software or hardware in the amount of time he was expecting. Jobs's team said he distorted their reality from pessimism (or some would say from realism) to optimism and, time and time again, they accomplished what they had thought was impossible. His belief was contagious and, as a result, Apple became one of the greatest companies on earth.

What could your team achieve if you shared your optimism and belief with each other and distorted reality?

Fear or Faith

Ultimately, being a positive team is all about working with faith in a world filled with cynicism, negativity, and fear. The ultimate battle we face every day is the battle between faith and fear.

As a team, you must realize that your members are facing this battle daily. They are filled with fear, doubt, and uncertainty, and it's your job to inspire them with faith. Remind each other that fear and faith have one thing in common—they both believe in a future that hasn't happened yet. Fear believes in a negative future. Faith believes in a positive future. If neither has happened yet, why wouldn't we choose to believe in a positive future? Why wouldn't we choose to believe our best days are ahead of us instead of behind us?

Tell your team that if you all believe your best days are behind you, that's the truth. If you all believe your best days are ahead of you, then that's the truth. Beliefs matter, so have faith in the future, work hard, and make it happen.

The Positivity Experiment

My friend, Kate Leavell, a former high-school lacrosse coach in Georgia, ran an experiment with her team to change the culture one season. Even though her previous teams had been winning, Kate wasn't enjoying coaching anymore, and her players' performance and effort levels were inconsistent. She knew the one area she struggled with the most was creating a positive team culture because she feared it would take away from the time they needed for training skills. She was also worried her team wouldn't take her seriously if she was too positive.

For the first time, she accepted winning as the by-product that it truly is, and focused all of her energy on building up her players and creating a positive team. She made a commitment to call out the good things she saw and put the mistakes into the practice plan so that she could correct them, rather than giving them negative energy that wouldn't help in the long run.

Instead of halftimes filled with corrections and blame, she gave feedback about what was going right and how they could use that to have a stronger second half. She still gave the team direction, but it was always framed in a way that communicated a firm belief in their ability to execute. At the end of every single game, win or lose, they had a celebration circle where the players gave each other positive shout-outs. Instead of focusing on mistakes, the primary focus was always centered on the positive of each interaction, play, and effort.

It wasn't long before the team began to mirror this approach with each other, and small huddles started to form on the field, where they would problem solve for themselves. Huddles began to form at practice too. The players were encouraging each other with positive feedback and direction, and they were getting excited about it.

The second half of every game, no matter how far behind they may have started out, shifted into thrilling comeback stories and record-breaking victories. A team that usually found themselves somewhere in the middle of the 70-team state ranking list closed in on a 12-game winning streak and finished in the top five as the regular season was wrapping up.

For the first time, they were playing for a state berth and the chance to enter the final four. With her team down 3–7 at halftime, it looked like the season and the experiment might be over. Kate stuck to her promise for the season to focus on positivity and let the team call out to each other the things that had brought them through tough situations in the past. That was all they needed; they knew what to do on the field, they just were struggling to execute it. They took the field after halftime full of belief in their ability and in each other, and they won that game 13–10, ultimately finishing third in the state that year. They broke every team record that season despite spending less time on drilling skills, taking more rests, and cutting out Saturday practices.

Kate's positive experiment demonstrates the truth that you don't have to choose between positivity and winning. Positivity leads to winning. Positivity leads to action, and action leads to results.

Don't Stop Believing

Jack Dorsey and his team at Twitter believed they had a great way for people to share information and communicate. Mark Zuckerberg's team at Facebook changed the way we connect with friends. Elon Musk's teams built the world's first electric sports car and launched rockets into outer space, despite countless obstacles and many moments where it seemed they would fail. Larry Page, Sergey Brin, and their team made Google into a verb, and transformed the way we search and find information. The team that produced and directed the movie *Black Panther* believed their movie could break down barriers and break through at the box office.

Every one of these teams faced adversity, challenges, resistance, negativity, and the real possibility of failure, but they overcame. Many writers and books focus on the great leaders that succeed, but we know it was the power of a positive team that created these life-changing and world-transforming technological and creative breakthroughs.

You and your team will face a lot of adversity, resistance, and negativity, but always remember that your certainty and optimism, belief and faith must be greater than all the negativity, fear, and doubt. Share your belief together as a team. Talk about it openly. Discuss your challenges and why you can overcome them. Confront the daunting tasks before you. Don't ignore them. Face them not with fear, but with faith.

Yes, you will face giants in your life that seem more powerful than you, but know and trust that they are no match for a team that refuses to give up. No matter what happens, don't stop believing.

The Best Is Yet to Come

A few years after Alan Mulally became the CEO of Ford, the economy went into a tailspin, the great recession hit, and the company faced the worst economic climate since the Great Depression. There were many moments where it looked like all the work Mulally and his One Ford team had done to restructure the company, build a united leadership team, create best-of-class automobiles, and become profitable was for naught. At the bottom of the recession when things looked the most bleak, the government bailed out Ford's competitors and the rules of the game seemed to change. Mulally and his team stayed positive about their plan and Ford's future. They believed the best was yet to come, and this belief and continued effort led to record profits and exponential growth in the future.

It also didn't look good for the Clemson football team when they trailed Alabama 14–7 at halftime in the 2017 national championship game, but as I looked around the locker room, I could tell no one doubted that they would win the game. They believed the best was yet to come.

I've worked with the Miami Heat the past three seasons. Last year, by the end of the first half of the season, they were 11–30, but the team refused to give up and continued to believe the best was yet to come. Their record for the second half of the season was 30–11 and coach Erik Spoelstra was a cowinner of the Michael H. Goldberg NBCA Coach of the Year Award from the National Basketball Coaches Association. The Heat didn't have a team of superstars, but they had players who believed in each other. They had a team that refused to let negativity sabotage them. They had a team that, despite their midseason record, believed the best was yet to come.

The Philadelphia Eagles lost their starting quarterback, Carson Wentz, to an ACL injury against the Rams during the 2017 season. Everyone thought and said their season was over, but the Eagles didn't listen to everyone. They stayed positive, believed in each other, rallied around their new quarterback, Nick Foles, and with relentless teamwork, faith, optimism, and determination, won an improbable Super Bowl.

Hopefully you see the pattern here. Great teams don't give in to the situation. They don't give up when things look bleak. They overcome the negative with positivity, belief, and optimism in order to be their best and bring out the best in others. A team that is positive and strong on the inside will overcome the negative forces they experience on the outside.

This brings us to an important point. Since a team will have to overcome the negative, they can't allow negativity from within to weaken them. A positive team can withstand the negative forces coming at them, but they will crumble if the negativity comes from within. Positive teams know and believe that outside forces cannot truly defeat them. They can only defeat themselves.

For a team to overcome the negative, it's essential to stay positive. We have discussed many ways to feed the positive, but now let's get real and talk about how to confront, transform, and remove the negativity that sabotages far too many teams.

Chapter 5

Positive Teams Transform and Remove Negativity

One of the most important decisions a team can make is to decide that they will not allow negativity to sabotage their team.

Being a positive team is not just about feeding the positive, but also about weeding out the negative. Positive doesn't mean Pollyanna. Negativity exists and you can't ignore it. One of the biggest mistakes teams make is that they ignore the negativity within their team. They allow it to breed and grow, and it eventually sabotages the team. You must address the negativity. Confront it, transform it, or remove it.

I remember getting a call in 2007, shortly after *The Energy Bus* was published, from Jack Del Rio, who was the head coach of the Jacksonville Jaguars at the time. A friend had given him the book; he read it and called to ask if I would meet with him. Keep in mind that I had just written the book. It wasn't in US bookstores yet. I had never worked with a sports team before, never mind a professional sports team, and I had never spoken to a leader of his stature before. I was very nervous.

Now, as I sat across from him he told me that he was allowing energy vampires to get to him and the book helped him realize that he needed to deal with the negativity. It also reminded him to be more positive than the negativity he was facing. He asked me to speak to the team, and for some reason I boldly said I would if he gave each player a copy of the book. He agreed. Most of the team read the book, I spoke to them about it, and thankfully they had an incredible season, making the playoffs for the first time in years. Players on the team talked to the media about being on the bus, feeding the positive dog, and not letting energy vampires sabotage the team. I didn't know it when I wrote it but after seeing what happened with this team I realized I had fortuitously written something that helped teams deal with negativity, and doing so was crucial to their success.

No Energy Vampires Allowed

One of the most important decisions a team can make is to decide that they will not allow negativity to sabotage their team.

In 2011 Mark Richt, the head football coach of the University of Georgia at the time, had his team read *The Energy Bus* and invited me to speak to them. I spoke before the season and, unfortunately, they lost their first two games. Georgia had been underperforming during the previous few seasons and the media was reporting that Richt was on the hot seat and would lose his job if this season didn't go well.

I texted him after the second loss and said, "I am sorry I didn't help more. I believe in this team. I believe you all are going to turn it around." Richt texted me back and said, "Jon, the guys are still on the bus. In years past we've allowed energy vampires to ruin this team but not this year. This year we won't allow it."

In the team meeting room, Richt had an artist draw a large picture of an energy vampire on the wall facing the seats where the players sit. If a player or coach acted like an energy vampire, the team took his picture from the media guide and put it on the wall. No one wanted to be on the wall. It was a message from Richt to his team that they would stay positive through their adversity and challenges.

The Power of a Positive Team

It worked, and the team went on to win the next 10 games in a row and made it to the SEC Championship.

It Starts at the Culture Level

I have found that the best way to address the problem of negativity on a team is at the culture level, where you set the expectation that people who drain the energy of others will not be tolerated. You talk about the detrimental impact of negativity. You explain that one person can't make a team, but one person can break a team. You talk about what a great culture looks like and how you want everyone to be a positive contributor to it. You make it clear what a great team looks like, and that it doesn't look like a bunch of complainers and blamers. You explain that it's unacceptable to be a source of negative energy that hurts the team. You build a culture so positive and strong that negativity can't breed, spread, and grow.

A school principal I know told me that she had some negative teachers on her team. She wasn't sure what to do at the beginning of the school year, but we told her to start with the culture and that will solve most of the problems. She wasn't convinced, but she focused on building a positive team and culture.

At the end of the year, one of the negative teachers came up to her and resigned. The negative teacher told her that the school was too positive and she couldn't take it anymore. She said that she felt like she was getting run over by positivity because no matter how much they wanted her to change she wasn't going to be positive.

When you feed the positive and create a culture where negative people are uncomfortable being negative, they will either

Positive Teams Transform and Remove Negativity

change or walk off the bus themselves. Whether they stay and become positive, or leave and stay negative, you will have improved your culture and moved your team in the right direction.

The First Step Is Transformation

What if you are trying to build a positive culture, but an energy vampire on your team is contaminating it? I receive this question often. The first step in dealing with an energy vampire is not to remove them, but to transform them.

No one really wants to be an energy vampire. These people are likely negative for a reason. The first steps should always be to listen with empathy and love, try to understand, and to coach and help them transform. Don't be negative about negativity. Don't sit in the dark with them. Instead, turn on the light.

For example, Martin, a leader with the company Seventh Generation, told me that he put a sign on his door that said: *Energy vampires welcome. Expect to be transformed.* He had a lot of great conversations and was able to transform a lot of negative energy into positive results.

Mark Richt also had a number of his players come to his office and tell him they weren't going to be energy vampires anymore. Several of the players from that team are thriving in the NFL, and quite a few others have become successful businessmen. It's rewarding to hear how the experience was a defining moment for a bunch of them.

Richt didn't kick these energy vampires off the bus. Instead, he confronted the negativity, invited them onto the bus, and sought to transform them—and it worked.

Remove the Negativity

But what if the energy vampires don't leave or change? What if they remain energy vampires and stay on the bus? I see this all the time. Not everyone is willing to change. No matter how much you try to help someone transform and grow, there will be some who are negative no matter what you do.

I heard from a school principal who invited her entire team onto the energy bus. She shared her vision for the road ahead and asked who was all in. All but two teachers bought in. She did everything she could to get those two teachers to be positive contributors. She documented and documented and documented her efforts (which she had to do for legal and personnel reasons), and eventually she had to let them off the bus. She told me that now they are on another bus somewhere else and her staff is feeling more positive and energized than ever. Two negative teachers were infecting their whole culture and mission to impact the lives of children. But since they were removed, the culture, morale, and energy have improved dramatically.

If transforming the negativity doesn't work, you must remove it. It doesn't sound positive, but it must happen sometimes for the good of the team. This doesn't mean you don't care about the negative person. It means you care about everyone else. You can still help the person as a friend or mentor. You just won't let them sabotage the team any longer.

If you are reading this and are one of the energy vampires, you can change and be more positive. I did and it made my team better—and I've seen a lot of people go from negative to positive and make their teams better.

If you are already positive, hopefully you and your team-mates can help transform a negative team member before it's too late. But regardless of where you are on the positivity or negativity continuum, know that one of your key roles as a team member is to create an environment where you and your team can do your best work.

It's Not Okay to Be Moody

One time I was visiting a college women's basketball team and they told me how they would often have to send one of the players home because she was in a bad mood and negatively affected the team. I asked if they had to do this with other players and they said there were several who were sent home occasionally. I then asked if these players were always in a bad mood. The coaches told me that they were positive sometimes and negative sometimes. Their moods fluctuated. They never knew what to expect and neither did their teammates.

When I spoke to the team that day I told them that it was important for them to be consistent. I challenged them to be positively contagious. I told them point blank that it's not okay to be moody. When you are moody, people around you don't know what to expect from you and this causes them to lose trust in you. I told them that no matter what is going on with school or your personal life, when you walk into the locker room or onto the court or the team bus, you have to decide to impact your teammates in a positive way.

To build a great team, you and your team members need to show up every day with a positive attitude. Focus on becoming the best version of yourself every day. Don't let negative circumstances and moods affect you and your team. Don't change depending on which way the wind is blowing; instead, be like a strong-rooted tree that does not waver, regardless of what is happening around it. Be the kind of consistent team member and team everyone knows they can trust and count on.

Implement the No Complaining Rule

One of the best ways to create a positive team environment and transform a toxic team culture is to implement the *no complaining rule.*

The no complaining rule says that you are not allowed to complain unless you have a solution to your complaint. This eliminates a lot of mindless and toxic complaining, and empowers you and your team to create solutions instead of focusing on problems. After all, if you are complaining, you're not helping. If you are complaining, you are focusing on where you are instead of where you want to be. Complaining causes you and your team to focus on everything except being your best. Complaining is like throwing up. Afterward you feel better but then the rest of your team is sick. It's toxic.

Rich Wilkerson's leadership team at Trinity Church in Miami implemented the no complaining rule and it had a dramatic impact on their leadership team. Then it spread to their volunteers and entire congregation, improving their culture in a very positive way.

I've also heard from hundreds of companies, schools, and teams that have transformed themselves with this simple, powerful, and practical rule. Dwight Cooper and his team at

PPR invented the no complaining rule and have not only been voted one of the best places to work each year, but have also seen incredible growth and profits. Mike Smith, the former head coach of the Atlanta Falcons, created a No Complaining Training Camp and saw improved morale and performance during training camp and throughout the season. Countless schools and hospitals have also implemented it with their teams, and it's amazing what happens when each person on a team decides to be a problem solver instead of a problem creator.

It's a really simple message and rule that guides you and your team to show up each day with a positive attitude and share positive energy instead of being energy vampires, complainers, and blamers. When you and your team focus on solutions instead of complaints, your performance rises to a higher level.

Weed and Feed

Michael Phelps and the US Olympic men's swim team is a great case study in feeding the positive and weeding the negative. When Phelps was interviewed by Bob Costas, he described their approach to building a positive team before the 2016 Olympics in Rio. He said:

> Every now and then you hear a bunch of negative comments or someone complaining, and during training camp at one of the meetings, I said to the guys that we are getting ready to go to the Olympics. This is what we have to do and if there is a negative comment, keep it to yourself. The more positivity we have as a team the better off we are

going to be. As soon as I said that we all became closer and then we really started getting going.

When I heard Michael say those words, I was thrilled because he shared a truth with the world that I have witnessed countless times throughout the years. A team with talent can be good. But they must come together to be great. Positivity is the glue that enhances team connection and performance, and it impacts office teams, school teams, church teams, and hospital teams as much as it does Olympic teams.

I've seen very positive teams with average talent accomplish more than anyone thought possible. I've also seen negative teams with a lot of talent accomplish far less than everyone thought was possible.

Positive teams work together more effectively. They stay positive, connected, and committed through challenges. They maximize each other's talent. They believe together and achieve more together. Positive, high-performing teams don't happen by accident. They are built by team members who reduce the negative and add a big dose of positive.

When you subtract negativity and add positivity to your talent, the sky is the limit. You must weed the negative and feed the positive. It's not a one-time thing you do at an annual meeting. You must consistently weed and feed and feed and weed to maximize the growth and potential of your team.

Positive Conflict

Let's be clear. Weeding the negative doesn't mean you eliminate disagreements. Positive teams are going to disagree. Great

73

teams fight. If you fight, it doesn't mean you are a negative team. Conflict is necessary to have a strong team.

While I've found that teams that have more positive interactions than negative interactions perform at a higher level this doesn't mean there should never be conflict. In fact, there needs to be some conflict. But why?

Well, all positivity and no conflict means that no one is asking the difficult questions. No one is discussing the important issues. No one is challenging the status quo. No one is challenging teammates to get better and no one is constructively criticizing others to improve. Having difficult conversations is key to being a great team as we will discuss later in the book.

Disagreeing with your team members doesn't make you an energy vampire. If your desire is to make the team better, sharing a complaint and offering a better way to do something doesn't make you a complainer. Constructively criticizing a team member doesn't make you a bad team member. You just need to make sure you do it in a positive way.

Kerri Walsh Jennings told me that she and volleyball partner Misty May-Treanor had disagreements, but they always talked them through. They never pointed the finger at each other or blamed one another.

Writing partners Brian Koppelman and David Levien have also disagreed, but not in a negative way. As part of the creative process, they share ideas and often ask one another, "But what about this?" They go back and forth, and once they agree on something, it's like yes, let's do that. They believe that you won't let your ego get in the way when your desire is to produce something great together. It doesn't matter whose idea it is. What matters is that they come up with the best idea.

I've found that positive conflict makes the team stronger if there is trust, respect, and love. If there's no trust, respect, and love, the conflict hurts the team. The problem is not the fighting. The problem is the lack of connection and relationship among the team members.

To be a great team and to engage in positive conflict, you need to trust each other and have a relationship. This leads us to the next principles that make great teams great. These principles go beyond a positive state of mind and require positive communication, connection, and action to create great relationships.

Chapter 6

Positive Teams Communicate and Connect

Everyone wants to be a great team, but to be a great team you must make the time to build great relationships.

Positivity is the glue in the process of building a powerful team, but to truly be a great team, you need to do more than just be positive. You need to communicate, connect, commit, and care to create meaningful relationships, strong bonds, and team unity.

The more I have worked with teams over the years, the more I realize that connection is the key. Just as Alan Mulally created One Ford by connecting his team and everyone in the company, you and your team must work together to be connected.

If you are part of a leadership team, doing this is essential for your organization because a team and organization that's not connected at the top crumbles at the bottom. I've worked with far too many organizations where the leadership teams are not connected. I can literally predict the success of a sports team based on how connected the owner, general manager, and head coach are. I can tell how well a business will weather challenges and grow by how unified and connected the leaders are.

I recently spoke at a meeting where two companies were merging together, and leaders from both companies were becoming one management group. We talked a lot about connecting and did some connection exercises, and you could see and feel the walls break down. Everyone who left the meeting felt that they would be much stronger going forward. Instead of two teams, they were now one team. I knew they were on their way to success because unity and connection are the difference.

I once sat in on a morning meeting of the leaders at Mercy Hospital in St. Louis. They were one of the most connected leadership teams I've ever witnessed. It was so powerful you could feel the connection. I was blown away. It was no surprise that their hospital was performing at a very high level.

You can have the greatest vision and purpose, but you must be connected and united in order to make it come to fruition.

Connection Is the Difference between Good and Great

Google is home to many of the most brilliant minds in the world, and a recent study called Project Aristotle released by the company revealed the keys to their most productive and inventive teams. Surprisingly, it was not team members' scientific knowledge but rather a connection between team members (generated by interest in teammates' ideas, empathy, and emotional intelligence) and also a feeling of emotional safety.

The connection you have with your team members creates a trust and a bond that allows you to be yourself and speak openly without worrying about being ridiculed. When team members are connected, have trust, feel emotionally safe, and feel like their ideas are being heard, they are able to do their best and most creative work.

As part of the study, Google found that although its A-teams were comprised of its top scientists, the company's most important and productive new ideas came from its B-teams, which were made up of people who weren't considered to be the smartest or most knowledgeable in the company. Google realized that great minds weren't the key to their success. It was great teams with a connection that freed their minds to create great inventions.

Project Aristotle proves what anyone who has been part of a team knows—connection is the difference between a good team and a great team. One of the biggest complaints I receive from leaders is that their teams aren't connected. They have a bunch of people who usually focus on themselves, their personal goals, their social media followings, and their egos. The message they receive from the world is that it's all about the individual, not the team. It's about *me*, not *we*.

Unfortunately, this may sound like your office and organization as well. There are a lot of silos, personal agendas, and office politics in all types of businesses and organizations.

The disease of *me* infects everyone. Narcissism and self-focus creates a disconnect between personal goals and team goals, and it undermines the team. People who put themselves and their projects before the team don't build great teams.

Through my work with teams, I have found that when people focus on becoming a connected team, the *me* dissolves into *we*. The individual silos come crumbling down, bonds are strengthened, trust is earned, relationships are developed, and the team becomes much more connected, more committed, and stronger.

You can't allow team members to stay isolated. You can't allow the disease of *me* to infect your team. It's important to create connection, trust, and emotional safety.

While visiting an NBA team a few years ago, I watched their game the night before I was to speak to the coaching staff. When I met with the coaching staff, they asked me what I saw. I told them I could tell there was a disconnect between some of the players. They couldn't believe it. They thought one of the coaches had told me what was happening behind the scenes, but I didn't need anyone to tell me.

When you work with enough teams and organizations you can tell who is connected and who isn't. You know when you see it and when you don't. It's the difference between an average team and a great team—and becoming a connected team begins with great communication.

It Starts with Communication

Communication starts the process of building a connected team. To connect with someone, you must communicate with them. Relationships are the foundation upon which great teams are built, and communication serves as the initial foundation in building a great relationship.

Communication builds trust. Trust generates commitment. Commitment fosters teamwork, and teamwork delivers results. Without great communication, you don't have the connection and trust to build a strong relationship. And without strong relationships, you can't have a strong team.

I had the opportunity to speak to Jimmie Johnson's racing team, and Chad Knaus, the crew chief and the most successful crew chief of all time, told me the difference between winning and losing—even living and dying, because auto-racing is such a dangerous sport—is his communication with Jimmie and the crew. The communication they have before and during a race, and the relationships they have created as a result of their communication, are keys to the success of their team—and they will be the keys to the success and survival of your team as well.

Where There Is a Void, Negativity Will Fill It

Most teams break down because of poor communication. In a world where we have more ways to communicate, we are communicating less meaningfully, and our relationships, teamwork, and overall engagement and performance are suffering.

Most people blame mobile phones for distractions, but it's not the phone. It's us. It's you and me. It's where you and your team members place your attention and intention. The more distracted you are, the less dedicated you will be. If you don't have communication, you won't have connection. If you don't have communication, you won't have the trust and commitment you need to build a great team and create the future together.

Even worse, I have found that where there is a void in communication, negativity will fill it. Without great communication, negativity fills the void and it breeds and grows, resulting in contagious negative energy that quickly spreads. Rumors, gossip, complaining, and negative energy all thrive when communication suffers.

When there is a void in communication, we assume the worst and act accordingly. We operate out of fear and try to survive instead of acting out of trust and a desire to help our team thrive.

Fill the Void

As a team you must make it a priority to fill the void through communication. It not only develops great relationships and trust, but it also prevents the spread of rumors and negative energy that can sabotage your team.

Communication is often the last thing you want to do, but it's the most important thing you must do. It won't happen by accident. You have to make time for it and be intentional about it. Find ways to communicate collectively as a team and also to foster one-on-one communication between team members.

The ways to enhance communication with your team are endless. At his company meeting, Dwight Cooper held a regular meeting at 8:31 A.M. every Monday morning to discuss challenges, weekly goals, and hot topics. I know of a sales team that holds a daily conference call to communicate obstacles, wins, and learning opportunities. I work with many companies that are made up of virtual business teams, and I advise them to establish a daily or weekly videoconference session with the team. You can also set a daily call at noon where a team leader or team member shares an inspirational message.

When I owned restaurants, I made it mandatory to have preshift meetings where the team would come together and talk about the keys to having a successful shift and to review key customer service strategies. I found the shifts went a lot more smoothly when we were all on the same page.

Speaking of restaurants, I think meals are a great time to communicate with different members, and I encourage people to eat with different members of their team each week to get to know each other better.

Regular meetings also work for families. When we held our family meeting each week to build our culture and talk about our vision and mission, it was also a great way to enhance our communication and connection. Things came up in these conversations that would have never come out if we didn't make time to intentionally communicate.

One-on-One Communication

You also want to make time for one-on-one communication. It doesn't have to be a long discussion, but frequent touch points and conversations are a great way to fill the void and avoid the spread of negativity.

School principal Windy Hodge told me that by communicating more with her teachers and fostering communication between her staff, teacher morale and performance improved dramatically.

One-on-one communication between team members is how you build a stronger team connection. Strong individual relationships help build a stronger team.

Why Don't We Communicate?

If communication and connection are so essential, then I must address why so many teams aren't more united and why we fall short in our effort to communicate.

I'm convinced that besides the fact that we don't recognize the value of communication, the enemies are busyness and stress. The research shows that when we are busy and stressed, we activate the reptilian part of our brain, which is associated with fear and survival. If you know anything about reptiles, you know that they will never love you. Reptiles are incapable of love because they are all about survival.

When we are busy and stressed, we activate our reptile brains and are focused only on survival. We are not thinking about uniting our teams and connecting with others. We are only thinking of how we can get through the day. As a result, we focus on what is urgent rather than what matters. We focus on our to-do list and how to survive rather than on our team and ways to thrive. We don't make the time to communicate and connect.

There's actually a scientific term for this: *cortical inhibition*. That is when the amygdala—the reptile brain—highjacks the neocortex, the part of the brain where you rationalize, make decisions, pray, practice gratitude, and love. I call the neocortex the positive dog part of the brain because of the loving nature of dogs.

When you are busy and stressed, your reptile, in essence, eats your positive dog. This is what has happened anytime you said something you regretted. Your reptile ate your positive dog, so you blurted out something mean, something that you would never say if you were thinking clearly. It's what happens during road-rage incidents. And it's what happens when team members fail to make time to connect with their teams.

The good news is that the research shows we have a quarter-second to override the reptile with our positive dog. We don't have to let the reptile win. We can understand that our enemies are busyness and stress, and we can learn to recognize when our reptile is coming alive (not unlike how Bruce Banner knows when the Hulk begins to emerge). We can take a deep breath when we realize we are getting stressed and find something to be thankful for in that moment. The research shows you can't be stressed and thankful at the same time.

And in each of these moments we can remember that our job is to communicate and connect, and not let the enemies conquer and divide. We can slow down and be more intentional in focusing on the relationships that truly build unity, connection, trust, and great teams.

When you know communication and connection are the keys, and busyness and stress are the enemies, you will slow down and make the time to communicate and develop great relationships.

On a Scale of 1 to 10

A great way to informally gauge how well you and your team are communicating is to have a team meeting and ask, on a scale of 1 to 10, how well you communicate as a team. A 10 means you communicate perfectly and a 1 means you barely know each other's name.

Having asked this question to numerous teams of all types I understand that the numbers are subjective and one person's 8 might be another person's 6. It's not a perfect science or measuring tool. The idea is to stimulate the team to think about how well or how poorly you communicate. I've also found that the overall numbers are pretty consistent and indicative of how well a team communicates.

Once everyone on the team shares their number, then the next question you should ask is, "Why isn't it a 10? Where do we fall short?" And then ask, "What would make it a 10?" This helps identify various voids in communication and leads to many great ideas and ways to improve team communication.

You can also do this individually as well. Have each person write their name on pieces of paper. Pass the sheets around and on the other side of the papers have each team member rate how well that person communicates, why they fall short of a 10, and what they could do to make it a 10. When everyone is finished rating one another, have each person read some of the reasons why they fall short, what they can do to improve, and what they will do to be a better communicator.

Listening Enhances Communication

People often think of communication as talking, but it's also listening and receiving feedback. The best communicator is not the person who is the most eloquent speaker, but the person who has the ability to listen, process the information, and use it to make decisions that are in the best interest of the team. The best listeners truly hear what their team is saying and trying to convey, and they strive to improve as a result. In *You Win in the Locker Room First* I shared how Mike Smith's greatest strength is the way he truly listens to his team and is open to their advice. It's no wonder that he won NFL Coach of the Year several times. Erik Spoelstra, Sean McVay, and Dabo

Swinney also won Coach of the Year as well, and I believe one of the reasons why is that they are all great listeners and learners. They listen to learn and they learn to grow. To be a great team you need to be people who listen to each other and learn from one another.

Communicate to Connect

Communication starts the process of building trust and connection, but if it remains superficial and involves small talk devoid of meaning, authenticity, and transparency, it won't lead to connection.

As a team you don't just want to communicate. You want to communicate *to* connect. When you communicate *and* connect, bonds are created, trust is developed, relationships are strengthened, and you become more committed.

Everyone wants to have a committed team, but you will never have commitment without connection. Connection is what leads to commitment. This is why connection is so important. It strengthens trust and creates a bond that leads to commitment.

Without connection, you will have a team that lacks commitment and underperforms. But with connection and commitment, your team will perform above its talent level.

Team Beats Talent When Talent Isn't a Team

The more connected you are, the more committed your team will be.

Before the 2013–14 college basketball season, I received a call from Billy Donovan, who at the time was the University of Florida basketball coach. (Now he is the head coach of the Oklahoma City Thunder.) Billy shared the challenges his team was facing and asked for my advice. I shared a few of my ideas with him and he immediately zoomed in on the concept of connection.

He said, "That's it, Jon. We often get to the Elite Eight but have trouble pushing through to the Final Four because we aren't as connected as we need to be. If we are more connected, we will have a better chance of winning the tight, big games."

Billy and I kept in touch during the season and I was blown away by all he did to connect with his players and foster relationships between them. I never saw a coach do more to invest in a team than what Billy did that season. The walls came crumbling down and, instead of a group of individuals, the Florida team became a connected family. They pushed through the Elite Eight to the Final Four and beat a very talented Kentucky team three times that season.

Despite the fact that not one person on their team was drafted into the NBA, Florida was able to beat teams with more talent because they were more connected. They are a great example of how team beats talent when talent isn't a team.

You may not have the most talented people on your team, but if you are a connected team, you will outperform many talented teams that lack a close bond. When teammates connect with each other, commitment, teamwork, chemistry, and performance improve dramatically.

Team + Talent

I learned from Brian Boland, who was the men's tennis coach at the University of Virginia, what happens when a team with talent also becomes connected.

Brian's team had just lost in an early round at the Intercollegiate Tennis Association Indoor Championships in Chicago. A blizzard had hit, so their flight home was canceled and they were stuck in their hotel. Brian had had enough. From 2001 to 2012 Brian had coached a lot of talented teams at UVA, but they could never seem to win a championship.

I previously shared how culture was a big part of their turnaround but it was, specifically, a culture of a connection that changed everything.

Brian gathered his team together in his room and asked them if they thought they were a connected team. They all said yes. Then he asked them who were the most important people in their lives. They all said their family. Then Brian asked if they knew anything about their teammates' families. It turned out they knew nothing about one another's families.

Brian asked them how in the world they could consider themselves a connected team if they knew nothing about the most important people in each other's lives. If you really know someone, shouldn't you know about what's important to them?

Now that the players' eyes and ears were wide open, Brian put the names of each team member in a hat and had each person pick one of the names. Each person had to learn about the family of the team member they picked from the hat. They

Positive Teams Communicate and Connect

had to call the player's family members and interview them, and also learn more about their teammate.

The players found out all sorts of things about their families and each other. Each teammate had to present to the entire team what they learned. Many family members submitted videos, and the experience was incredible. Brian said it was the most powerful thing he has ever done.

It must have been powerful because they won the national championship that year and three of the next four years after that. For 12 years Brian couldn't win a championship, then he won four out of five before leaving to lead USTA Men's Tennis. When I asked him why UVA had succeeded, he said, "I became a different coach and we became a different team." In addition to the family exercise, he said they also often sat around a table and would openly talk about the team, the challenges they were facing, and all sorts of issues and topics.

I asked him what he did if a player wasn't interested in engaging in these kinds of talks. What if he said, "I just want to play tennis"? Brian said that wasn't an option. If a guy seemed disengaged, he and the staff would meet with him and find out why and get to the bottom of the issue.

He never had someone leave the UVA team. They conformed to the culture, learned to connect, and became committed to the team in the process. When he's asked how he has won so many championships, he says, "Our love for each other is the difference."

In other words, the trust and bond formed through connection leads to a greater commitment that when combined with talent leads to championships.

Team Building

As Brian's example demonstrates, connection doesn't happen by accident. In a world where we're more virtually connected than ever, it seems that our teams are more disconnected than ever. Too many teams don't make the time to invest in relationships and team building. They work on individual skills but too often fail to develop the chemistry and relationships that truly build great teams.

Positive, high-performing teams are built and developed through great communication, shared experiences, positive interactions, common challenges, and vulnerable storytelling that connect people at a deeper level.

Navy SEALs are famous for their team-building work, where a difficult shared experience creates a bond. I love their work and admire them greatly, but as I tell my friends who are SEALs, I don't think you have to jump in a cold ocean together and only sleep a few hours a night to create a bond.

Exercises that cause people to be vulnerable, transparent, and authentic cause the walls of pride and ego and selfishness to come crumbling down and lead to strong connections and meaningful relationships. You and your team must make time for these types of team-building exercises to foster communication, connection, and commitment.

In this spirit, I'd like to share a few of my favorite team-building exercises to create more connection and commitment. Note: I'm a proponent of a weekly team-building session, but you can find a rhythm that works best for you. Whatever you do, just don't make it a one-time, beginning-of-the-year event. It won't last. You have to be intentional and build your team throughout the year. Please know that it's always a little awkward at first for any of these exercises. Many people are not used to being vulnerable. But I've found that, after the first few people, the energy shifts quickly.

1. **If you really knew me.** If you really knew me you would know this about me: _____.
I recently took a leadership team through this exercise and, at first, they shared very shallow comments like "you would know that I'm very generous and wonderful." But after challenging them to go deeper and sharing something vulnerable about myself, they started sharing meaningful stories and feelings that connected the team in a deep and powerful way. (Thanks to my friend Mike Robbins for the idea.)

2. **Share a defining moment.** Stand in a circle or sit at round tables and have each team member share the story of a defining moment in their life, one that helped them become who they are today. When you do this, you'll learn things you never knew before. Immediately, you'll know your team members a whole lot better and feel more connected to them. It's amazing how simple and powerful this exercise is.

3. **The Safe Seat.** Dabo Swinney, the head coach of the Clemson University football team, told me about a stool his friend brought him from a remote fishing village. He said guys would sit on these stools in a circle and talk about life, family, fishing, and so on.

It gave Dabo an idea and he called it the Safe Seat. He placed the stool in the team meeting room and, after each practice, a different teammate sat on the Safe Seat while the team gathered around in a circle. Dabo then asked the teammate questions about his life, family, and a defining moment. When Dabo was finished asking questions, the rest of the team was free to ask questions.

The stool was called the Safe Seat because it was a safe place for each person to share his story and heart with his team. It was a safe place to be vulnerable, knowing that whatever was shared while sitting on the stool would not leave the room. It was a safe spot in a safe room.

As each teammate took their turn in the Safe Seat, the players began to know each other a whole lot better. And as Dabo said, it was a big factor in his team's rise to success.

4. **The Triple H: hero, highlight, hardship.** I learned this one from Cori Close, the UCLA women's basketball coach. Each person talks about one of their heroes and shares why they admire them. Then the players share a positive highlight as well as a hardship from their past. The Richmond Football Club won the AFL (Australian rules football) championship for the first time in 36 years and the team credits this exercise for developing the trust, connection, and commitment that led to their incredible season. In the book *Yellow and Black* by Konrad Marshall the players share how the triple H sessions they did not only changed their team, but also had a huge impact on their lives.

5. **The Hard Hat.** As a team, discuss and identify the characteristics of a great team member. What does it mean to be a great team member? Write all the characteristics on a board, or wall. Have each person choose the one that resonates most with them and share with the group how they will be a great team member. Visit HardHat21.com for 21 ways to be a great teammate.

6. **Get on the bus together.** A lot of teams read *The Energy Bus* to create unity and a common dialogue, but some teams go a little deeper. For example, one business leader I know paired up the people on her team and had each pair present to the rest of the team one of the ten rules of *The Energy Bus* in a fun and creative way. Some made a video, some sang a song, some gave a speech, some created a skit. She said it brought the rules to life and they connected with each other in the process.

7. **One word.** Have each team member choose one word that will help drive them to be their best and bring out the best in others. You may choose a word such as: connect, commit, serve, give, help, care, love, tough, relentless, excellence, selfless, and so on. Then have each team member share their word with the team and explain why they chose it.

8. **Ten questions.** Make up a list of 10 questions. During each team-building session, have each person pair up with a different team member, ask each other the questions, and share their answers. This will help you get to know your team members and become more connected.

It's a great exercise for sports teams to do when they are on the bus or plane heading to a game. It's also great for all teams to do once a week or once a month, depending on how many people you have on the team.

9. **Game dynamics.** My friend Steve Shenbaum has created an entire business where he helps executives, military members, athletes, and teams improve through game dynamics. Steve has teams play games rooted in competition and humor. He said the experience of doing something unfamiliar (like having three people form the shape of an elephant) together while competing and laughing really bonds a team together. I can tell his games have a big impact because I see Steve each year at the Pittsburgh Pirates spring training facility, and players always come up to him and give him a hug.

It's Worth It

It takes time and energy to connect with your team. You may have to sacrifice other things, but it's well worth it. I recently heard from Pam Bates, the general manager of Galva Family Dentistry. She said, "We have begun having one-and-a-half-hour weekly meetings with our dental team. We committed to these meetings and knew we were taking production hours away from the dental practice. It was a risk, and we wondered if this time would be productive every week! It's been amazing. We are developing and improving our systems in the office. One of the best team-building activities at each meeting is a vulnerability question that everyone has to answer (no passes). It may have to do with their past struggles or successes, what scares them, inspires them, and so on. There have been tears and laughter in this process! Learning about your team members can really help you understand them. This has also gotten everyone to be more open to share in the development of our systems, and we are thriving."

Making time to connect is always worth it. Before the 2016 season, I spoke to the Los Angeles Dodgers at their spring training facility about the importance of being a connected team and, over the past two seasons, I have witnessed the power of these connections.

One day while I was sitting in manager Dave Roberts's office, one of his players walked in to say hello. Dave got up from his chair and gave the player a big bear hug for about five seconds. It was the kind of hug that a dad would give his son after returning home from a long trip. They talked for a little bit about life and practice before the player said, "I'll see you later," and left.

I told Dave how great it was that he would give his player a hug like that. He said, "I do it each day and he often stops by to talk about life and challenges and whatever is on his mind."

A few weeks later, while watching the Dodgers play in the postseason, I watched in amazement as this player hit several home runs to help the Dodgers advance. It was as if I had a front-row seat to see the impact of what happens when a coach makes the time to pour love and support into one of his players. This player who had struggled was now one of the heroes because his leader took the time to connect with and care about him.

Before the World Series this year, I walked with Dave to the field to watch the team practice. After a few minutes of talking with me, Dave said, "I have to go connect with my players, Jon." I then watched Dave as he connected with each player one on one. I heard it was something that A.J. Hinch, the manager of the Houston Astros, did as well. It was no surprise then that two teams with managers who believed in the power of connection, and made time to act on it, would be playing in the World Series together.

It takes a lot more time and energy to connect, but the team and results it produces are well worth the effort.

Team Grit

Even though I've been sharing success stories of positive and connected teams, I know that being a positive and connected team doesn't always mean you will win championships, have record sales numbers, win awards, or succeed with your new design or product. There are a lot of other factors that are involved that can determine your fate. But being positive and connected does mean that you won't give up, because you will have team grit.

Angela Duckworth, the foremost researcher and expert on grit, writes and speaks a lot about individual grit, but when I asked her if there was much research on team grit she said there wasn't. I told her my theory and experience that, in addition to teams having a shared vision, greater purpose, collective optimism, and belief, the bond and relationships they have is a big factor in determining the level of team grit.

If you love your team, you won't give up on them. The more connected you are, the more committed you will be. If you are committed to each other, you will fight *for* each other,

Positive Teams Communicate and Connect

not *with* each other. You will move forward together through failure, adversity, and challenges.

I've found that the grittiest teams are the most connected and committed to each other. Since connection and commitment are essential to building a gritty team, I want to discuss ways to further enhance your team's connection and commitment. It's really simple and it includes team members who commit and care.

Connection and commitment both rise when all members of the team commit themselves to the team and show they care. When you commit and care, you take your connection, commitment, and team grit to an even higher level. In this spirit, let's talk about how positive teams commit and care.

Chapter 7

Positive Teams Commit and Care

When we *comes before* me, *you become the person and team you are meant to be.*

For every Academy Award winner, there is a team of writers, set designers, sound technicians, and production crew members that made the award possible. For every Super Bowl–winning quarterback, there's a center, an offensive line, receivers, an offensive coordinator, trainers, coaches, and a support team that lead the way to the championship. For every new automobile, there's a team of designers, suppliers, engineers, and quality testers that make it possible for drivers to get behind the wheel.

In most of these cases we know about the superstar, the award winner, the team leader, the celebrity CEO, the champion coach, but we don't hear about the selfless team and crew that works countless hours and gives their sweat, tears, and years to the team and cause. We see the star on stage but we don't see all the people who committed themselves selflessly to the team to allow the star to shine. But just because we don't hear about them doesn't mean they aren't valuable. In fact, it is their selflessness, sacrifice, and commitment to the team that makes the team great.

Every great team has team members who commit themselves to the team. It is each individual's commitment to the team that leads to collective greatness. The truth is, if you want to be a great team, you and your team members must commit to the team.

Play Your Notes

Marching bands and drum corps are great examples of the commitment needed to be a great team. Shaun Gallant, the director of programs for Vanguard Musical and Performing Arts and the six-time world champion Santa Clara Vanguard Drum and Bugle Corps, told me the importance of everyone's role in the band to compete at the highest level. Each member must not only perform music but they are marching very quickly (200 steps per minute) in every direction, and sometimes even dancing.

For marching bands to perform at their highest level, each member of the band needs to be excellent in their own music and movement and trust that each member is doing their part so the movement and music is in sync. They must commit themselves to the music and to each other. Chris Parks, the director of athletic bands at Stony Brook University, added that when there is commitment and trust by all members of the team, the band is able to create music that energizes and inspires.

It's no wonder we love music. After all, we live in the universe. Universe means "One Song." We are living in the one song. We are instruments that create the symphony of life. Harmony results when all people play their own notes to create a beautiful sound together.

A team works the same way. When each person plays their note and commits to the team, they are able to create great music together.

Team First

My friend Nick Hays is a former Navy SEAL who now works with many professional sports teams and businesses. He told me that Hell Week is the single most influential point in the forging of a young Navy SEAL because it drives home a team-first mentality.

Nick shared that in BUD/S (Basic Underwater Demolition/ SEAL training) a class of people who wish to become SEALs go through more than six months of rigorous selection. A couple of weeks into BUD/S, they participate in the much-dreaded Hell Week. During this week, the students will run over 200 miles, carry boats and logs, and spend most of their time wet and on the verge of hypothermia, while getting only two to four hours of sleep total between Sunday morning and Friday afternoon.

Nick said the number of people who quit during that week is staggering. I asked Nick when most of the SEALs quit, and he told me:

Most people quit between the beginning of [Hell Week] until Tuesday night. After Tuesday people do not quit. They will sometimes get injured and be unable to finish, but they will not ring the bell (our outward expression of quitting). Why is that?

When you begin the week, you are excited. You have prepared for this, you have seen it in movies or read about it in books. You want to see if you can pull it off. You want to become a Navy SEAL. See a trend here? *You, you, you.* When the student is thinking of themselves, they imagine themselves for the next five days of no sleep, utterly fatigued and cold to the bone.

That is a lonely place to be. I saw it more than once. The sun was going down behind the freezing water on the horizon. The person next to me refused to walk forward to

Positive Teams Commit and Care

the water. He stepped back while everyone else stepped forward. He could no longer imagine himself stretched to the very limits for another four days. Then it happens.

Someone who once bragged they would die before they quit is standing in front of his peers and ringing a bell. Leaving his team to go back to the warmth of a bed. This person was focused on themselves. They were able to do some good things but eventually found a plateau that they could not break through—a problem that they could not outrun—and their resolve broke.

I was fortunate to see things differently. I was placed in a boat crew, with seven other guys. Together, we would carry boats and logs while covered in wet sand. When racing other boat crews, we would fire each other up with praises and motivation. Later, in the ocean, we would link arms together in the water for what seemed like forever. To pass the time, we would sing songs and tell jokes. During meal times, we would laugh at each other. There was a bond forming.

I did not think about myself at the end of the week—about how far I had to go, or how bad it might get. Believe me, I was not an exceptional athlete and every day was a battle, but I knew that my team needed me here and now. My team needed me to run as fast as I could in the next race. I was needed to lighten the mood when the night felt cold and long. I was no longer fighting for myself; I was fighting for my boat crew and for the man at my side. I was more afraid of letting them down than I was of being cold, wet, and miserable.

We had become a team. The power of that team was unstoppable. It was bigger than any one person, dream, or history.

The Power of a Positive Team

On Friday morning, more than five days since we had laid down in a bed, we lined up on the beach ready to walk into the freezing water yet again. Just before we hit the water, the instructors told us to turn around. On top of the sand berm was a large American flag and all of our family and friends. "Hell Week is secure," the instructor said over the loudspeaker.

Just like that, it was over. The beginning of that week felt like a lifetime ago. I was a different man now. At the beginning of the week, I had hopes, dreams, and aspirations. At the end I had commitment and a purpose. I had a team.

It's incredible what happens when you commit to your team. As Nick shared, you do things you never thought you could on your own. You make the team better and yourself better in the process. When *we* comes before *me*, you become the person and team you are meant to be.

We before *Me*

I know the power of *We* before *Me*. I saw my dad live it every day as a New York City police officer. He and his partner were like brothers because every day they put their lives on the line for each other. They were a great team because they were committed to each other and focused more on their partnership and protecting each other rather than their own survival. They knew that working for each other made them stronger than working for themselves.

Brian Koppleman said that one of the keys to his successful partnership with his writing partner David Levien was their mutual commitment to each other. He said, "We had tremendous

Positive Teams Commit and Care

trust because we knew that our united interest was more important than our self-interest. During our down moments we picked each other up. We never blamed the other guy. We encouraged each other and recognized when each other did something great. We never told the outside world who did what or who wrote what line. We did everything together, regardless of whose idea it was. Neither of us had an ego and neither one of us wanted to receive credit individually. Our partnership was and is so strong that we would fall on a sword for each other."

I also saw the concept of *we* before *me* embodied in the Los Angeles Rams. I met with their new head coach, Sean McVay, a month before the start of training camp. We discussed many principles and ideas for building a great team and, when I mentioned *we* before *me*, Sean laughed because it was something he had already written down and decided was going to be one of his key messages to the team.

He asked me to speak during training camp to reinforce the message, which I did, and it has been exciting to watch the team embody this principle. I know they have embodied it because Sean and his staff have modeled it through their incredible leadership, and the players on the team have put team success before their own individual accomplishments. At their practice facility you'll see "We not Me" painted on the walls, but more importantly you will see it lived on the practice field, in the locker room, and in the stadium on game day.

It's no wonder they won their division with an 11–5 record, compared to their dismal 4–12 record the season before. It's also no surprise the Philadelphia Eagles won the Super Bowl. They were a positive, powerful, and talented "We before Me" team that had a supernatural bond that lead to extraordinary commitment.

Commitment Recognizes Commitment

When a team member changes their focus from *me* to *we* it has an amazing impact on the team. Steve Johnson, arguably the best college tennis player of all time, had helped his team win three national tennis championships in a row. He had the opportunity to turn pro and make a few million dollars on the tour. He could have easily left to pursue his own greatness, but Steve was more concerned with the greatness of his team. He decided to stay at the University of Southern California (USC) to help his team win a fourth championship.

USC tennis coach Peter Smith told me he still remembers standing on a sandy beach with his team as they looked at the icy-cold water of the Pacific. They were about to do a team-building session with former Navy SEALs before the start of the season. When the Navy SEALs arrived, they all wanted to know who Steve Johnson was, and when they found out they walked over to shake his hand. They had heard about his decision to return to the team to help them win a fourth championship. They knew how much money he had given up to do so, and they wanted to meet the man who was so committed to his team.

I got goosebumps when Peter told me this story. Some of the most committed people on the planet, Navy SEALs, recognize and appreciate commitment, and they saw it in Steve's commitment to his team.

In hearing this story, I realized that commitment recognizes commitment. When you live it, you see it in others. I also realized that commitment also fosters commitment, as it did with Steve's teammates. They knew he was committed to their team and it was Steve's commitment that inspired an even greater commitment from them.

Positive Teams Commit and Care

Steve was only responsible for 35 percent of the team's points for any given match, so when you look at USC's four national championships in a row you know that Steve didn't do it alone. They did it as a committed team. It was Steve's commitment to his team and their commitment to Steve and each other that lead to their winning a fourth championship.

Committing Makes Everyone Better

What I love most about commitment is that, through your actions, you not only make your team better, but you also get better in the process. No one illustrates this point more than Swen Nater.

Swen Nater was an All-American basketball player at Cypress Community College when UCLA coach John Wooden recruited him. As the story goes, Wooden said that Nater wouldn't play in a lot of games because UCLA already had the best center in the world, Bill Walton, but Nater would have the opportunity to play against Walton every day in practice.

Wooden wanted the six-foot-eleven Nater to challenge and push Walton to improve. Nater accepted his role during his time at UCLA and every day in practice he focused on one task: making Walton better.

While he was helping Walton improve, something interesting happened. Nater also improved. He was the only player in ABA and NBA history to be drafted in the first round having never started a collegiate game. Nater was named the ABA Rookie of the Year and went on to have a 12-year career in the ABA and NBA.

Nater is a great example that when you commit yourself to make the team better, you also get better. When you focus on helping others improve, you improve. When you lose your ego in the service of others, you find the greatness within you. Great teammates serve their team members. Great teams commit to serve each other.

There are countless ways to help others improve. I can't tell you what you should do, but I can tell you that when you commit to your team, you will be well on your way to building a great team.

Serve to Be Great

When I'm in Los Angeles I go to Mosaic on Sundays. It's considered one of the most diverse churches in America and each week you'll find people from a variety of ethnic backgrounds, races, and faiths in attendance.

I recently spoke to their leadership team, made up of mostly volunteers, and learned that when someone wants to get involved with the church and help with music, volunteer projects, parking, or any leadership role, they must first serve. One of Mosaic's pastors, for instance, served as the janitor for a few years before he ever took the stage to preach. And even a famous actor/singer who wanted to sing in the band first had to serve the band coffee before he would be allowed to join them on stage. I realized they were a great leadership team because they committed to the team by serving each other.

Great teams don't have people who serve themselves. They have people who serve the team and each other. They have people who are willing to sacrifice themselves and what they want for the good of the team.

People often ask me what committing looks like. I say it always looks like service and sacrifice. It looks like doing what the team needs rather than what you want as an individual. I asked a school principal, football coach, and business leader when their team became a powerful team. They all said it happened when we served each other instead of ourselves.

Commit to Your Team

Earl Watson, like Swen Nater, also played at UCLA and was mentored by John Wooden. After playing in college he had a successful career in the NBA. One day his college teammate, Billy Knight, who had struggled to make an NBA team, asked Earl why he thought he was having trouble making it in the NBA. Billy wanted to know Earl's secret. Earl told him to practice playing pick-up at the UCLA gym and figure out how to win without scoring.

Billy was only focused on shooting and scoring, and Earl knew that to be a great teammate he had to find other ways to make his team better. Earl encouraged Billy to not shoot at all and instead work on rebounding, setting screens, passing, defending, and, most importantly, vocally empowering his teammates by saying things like: *Great shot. Let's go. Keep shooting. I believe in you. I knew you would make it happen. I can feel it.*

Earl said that if you can help your teams win without scoring, you will be ready for the NBA. That's what Earl did every off-season to prepare for another NBA season. His secret was his commitment to making his team better.

When you commit to your team, you not only make them better but *you* also get better. When you help others improve, you improve. When you help your team grow, you grow.

Do You Care?

At the end of the day, communicating, connecting, committing, and becoming a great team won't happen unless you care. Caring underlies every principle in this book. After all, if you don't care, you won't make the time to communicate, encourage, connect, commit, serve, or sacrifice.

Great teams care about their team. They care about the work they do. They care about communicating and connecting with one another. They care about each other, so they commit to one another. They care about their performance. They care about what they are producing as a team. Because they care, they do more, give more, encourage more, help more, mentor more, develop more, build more, and, ultimately, accomplish more.

To be a great team you must care about your team and the work you are doing together. If you care, you'll make time to communicate. You'll put in the effort to connect. You'll sacrifice to commit. You'll go above and beyond for each other and you'll often accomplish more together.

I can't make you care as a team, but I can tell you that if you don't care, you won't be great. I can tell you that caring is one of the greatest success strategies of all and the teams that care greatly are the ones that produce great work and leave a lasting legacy.

In Walter Isaacson's biography of Steve Jobs, Isaacson shared a story about Jobs as a young boy helping his father

Positive Teams Commit and Care

build a fence. His father told him he must care about crafting the back of the fence as much as the front. When Steve asked why the back mattered when no one would see how it was crafted, his father said, "But you will know."

Steve's father taught him to care more and, years later, he and the design team at Apple went on to create Apple products with such care that they generated feelings of awe, loyalty, and passion among the brand's millions of new customers. It wasn't an accident. Jonathan Ive, the man who has designed many iconic Apple products, said, "We believe our customers can sense the care we put into our products."

The team at Apple cared about the work they did and the products they created and, in turn, their customers cared about them. Their care created products that changed the world and left a legacy.

Care More

Kathy Norton cared. She cared a lot. She cared *more*. She was an insurance adjustor for one of my clients, Gallagher Bassett, and while working with one of her clients she found out she had cancer and didn't have long to live.

You would think that she would have left her job to stay at home or travel and see places on her bucket list, but Kathy cared more about her clients than any of that. In her job, she handled workers' compensation claims, so her job was to help people rehab, heal, get back on their feet, and put their lives back together. She cared so much about the people she was working with that she couldn't leave them or her job. So she spent the last few months of her life caring about and helping her clients.

Cindy Kincannon, the associate manager of claims for Kathy's client, worked closely with Kathy. Even though they worked for separate companies, they operated as one team to serve Cindy's company's employees if they were injured on the job. Cindy said that her team has been forever impacted by Kathy's care, and her commitment to her clients.

Kathy's team at Gallagher Bassett was also deeply impacted by her. After her death, her team got together and decided they were going to care more like Kathy Norton. As a result, they've become a model for the rest of the company.

I'm sure you care. You wouldn't be reading this if you didn't care. But I want to encourage you to care more like Kathy Norton.

Craftsmen and Craftswomen

Positive team members see themselves as craftsmen and craftswomen instead of carpenters. There's a difference between a carpenter and a craftsman. A carpenter just builds something but a craftsman puts in more time, energy, effort, and care to build a work of art. Instead of just showing up and going through the motions, a craftsman works to build masterpieces. In a world where too many settle for mediocrity, craftsmen and craftswomen seek to create excellence and build greatness. They care more and, because they care more, they invest more—more energy, effort, sweat, tears, and years mastering their craft.

While speaking to a leadership team, I asked them how many believed they could work harder than they already were. Everyone raised their hands. Then I said, "So what's the next question?" They answered, "Why aren't you?" We discussed it and decided that to work harder, you have to care more.

If you care more, you will put your heart, soul, spirit, and passion into your team. If you care more about your project, work, and craft than about all the distractions vying for your attention, you won't allow those distractions to get in the way. You will invest your energy into building something meaningful that lasts.

Positive teams are made up of craftsmen and craftswomen who care more and, as a result, they create more masterpieces.

You Can't Fake It

Your team knows if you care or not. You can't hide it and you can't fake it. You can't decide to care because the book says so or so you can check a box. Caring comes from the heart. That's why we say things like: *She puts her heart into her work. He put his heart and soul into it. She has a big heart. Do it with all your heart.*

Caring is an outward expression of what's inside a person's heart. If your heart isn't into it, your team will know. If your team doesn't care, the world will know.

When you walk into a restaurant, you can very quickly tell if the staff cares or not. When you eat your meal, you can tell if the chef and cooks care. When you go to your dentist's office, you can tell if the dental team cares. When you walk into a school, you can tell if the team of educators care.

As Jonathan Ive noted, people can tell the care that is put into something. Mark Zuckerberg said that Facebook became what it is because he and his team were the ones who cared enough to make it work.

I buy my suits from Rosenblums because I know they care. I go to Johnny Cuts to get my hair cut because Johnny cares. I've stopped doing business with people when I know they don't care. We buy products from teams that care. We use services from teams that care. We love and support teams that care.

If you and your team don't care, then discuss why, address the issues, identify a solution, and get back to caring. Your team will do your best work when you care, and your team will thrive because of it.

Chapter 8

Positive Teams Are Always Striving to Get Better

Positive teams don't just have fun together. They pursue greatness together. They believe the best is yet to come so they give their best to create the best outcome.

A team that cares does more than commit to each other. They also commit to getting better for each other.

From 431 to 371 BC, the Spartans were the premier fighting force in Greece and perhaps the world. Despite the fact that they existed almost 2,500 years ago, they are still wildly popular in our culture and we see them on TV and in movies all the time.

Why were they so great? Former Navy SEAL Nick Hays said, "It's because their *culture* valued the tactics and mind-set necessary to fight together as a single-minded unit. The Greek hoplite phalanx was a battle formation made up of heavily armed foot soldiers who moved in very tight ranks. Soldiers using this strategy relied on the strength of the shields of the men to their left and right. The individual warrior saw it as his *job* to keep his shield up and to stay alive so that he could stay in the fight. Staying in the fight meant that he could do his job and enable his team members to do their jobs."

A team that cares is made up of people who do their job to be the best they can be for themselves and their team. They pursue excellence and are always looking for ways they can learn, improve, and grow. They are humble and hungry and willing to be uncomfortable. They don't settle. Instead they always challenge the status quo and chase greatness.

Great teams aren't born. They are made up of individuals who are always striving to get better, who pursue excellence and make their team members better.

The One Percent Rule

It's a simple rule I share with teams to help them create excellence. The rule says to give one percent more time, energy, effort, focus, and care today than you gave yesterday. Each day, give more than you did the day before.

Obviously you can't calculate one percent, but you can push yourself more today than you did yesterday. You can improve and get better today. You can strive for excellence and work to become your best. You can tune out distractions and focus even more on what matters most.

I worked with a college women's lacrosse team of 35 players who were all implementing the one percent rule. They said if each person gives one percent more each day that's 35 percent daily and, over time, this extra percent will produce big results. It did. They had incredible growth by pursuing both individual and team excellence.

Own the Boat

My friend Marilyn Krichko helps hundreds of teams of all types each year through her rowing team-building programs. She gets a team together in a boat on the water, and they have to learn to row together.

One of Marilyn's key tenets is "Everyone on the team *owns the boat* and is responsible for what happens." It is each member's responsibility to take action to improve the performance of the team.

I love the visual of a crew in a boat all rowing in unison together. It's a great metaphor for all teams. Each person must row to the best of their ability but they must also row in unison with their team and make the team better in the process. Each person must do their job and excel at their role, and when they do that, they improve the performance of the team.

As you strive to be your best, you bring out the best in your team. One person in pursuit of excellence raises the standards and performance of everyone around them. And when you have a team all doing their job, excelling in their roles and pursuing excellence together, the sky is the limit.

Elite of the Elite

I met a leader of Special Forces for the United States and he told me about the selection process for SEAL Team Six. While Navy SEALs are considered to be elite members of Special Forces, they have to try out to be members of the elite SEAL Team Six unit.

He said that while prospects are trying out, the current members of SEAL Team Six look for certain characteristics. If during the tryout a prospect doesn't fit their criteria, SEAL Team Six says, "Thank you very much, but you're not the right fit."

"What's the right fit?" I asked.

He said, "What we are looking for is not just someone who performs at the highest level but who, while performing at the highest level, also looks out for his team members, making them better in the process."

Positive Teams Are Always Striving to Get Better

It occurred to me that if you want to be elite, you can be a high performer, but if you want be *the elite of the elite*, you have to be a transformational positive team member—someone who makes others better in the process. To be a great team, you not only want to do your job well, but also help your team members do their jobs better.

Love and Accountability

Two words are the two most important keys to making your team better: love and accountability. After all, it's not easy to get a crew to work together. Sometimes a team member isn't on their game. Sometimes they don't seem like they care. Sometimes they don't seem like they are giving their best effort.

One of the most frequent questions I receive is how to get a team member motivated to give 100 percent. As we discussed, it starts with each team member giving 100 percent themselves. Do your job. Own the boat. Lead by example. Speak through your actions. As Benjamin Franklin said, "Well done is better than well said."

The next step is to make sure your team members know that you love them. If you love them and they know it, you will earn the right to challenge and push them. Too many teams try to motivate through demands and rules, but that only leads to oppression not inspiration. Andy Stanley said rules without relationships lead to rebellion. Rules are fine but without love and relationships, team members will rebel, burn out, or disengage. That's why *we before me* is such a powerful principle.

We often talk about holding our team accountable, but if teammates truly love each other, they'll want to be their best for each other. I've found that the more team members love each other, the fewer rules they need. Because they love their team members they don't want to let them down. A team driven by love, not rules, will be more accountable to each other. Of course, this doesn't mean accountability shouldn't be a part of your team.

The best teams have a combination of love and accountability. Love drives the relationship, while accountability to the culture, values, principles, expectations, and standards of excellence moves the relationships toward greatness. In other words, you and your team are united by love to do something great together. You are not here to just hang out together. You are here to do something meaningful and produce something amazing together. You love each other and hold each other accountable to a higher standard. You are a family and a great team.

Family and Team

We often say that we want our team to be like a family. But just because you are like a family, doesn't mean you are a great team.

Coach Hank Janczyk and his Gettysburg College lacrosse team won 20 straight games a few seasons ago. When I asked him what happened, he said, "You know, Jon, I realized that, before the season, we were a family. We loved and cared about one another. We had strong bonds and great relationships. But we weren't a great team. Our guys made excuses for each other. They covered for each other when a teammate didn't do the right thing. They loved hanging out together, but they didn't bring out the best in each other on the field." Hank knew they couldn't just be a great family. They had to also become a great team—and add accountability to the love that they had.

The same issue has come up for a number of my corporate teams. For example, as I was preparing to speak at an annual leadership meeting for a large family-owned company, I asked the leadership to share their biggest challenge. They said, "We have such a wonderful family culture and it's what makes us special, but it's also a challenge for us to hold each other accountable as we grow."

I told them what I tell your team now: Just because you are a family doesn't mean you are a great team. To be a great team, you hold each other accountable, not to rules but to a standard of excellence. You challenge each other to improve and make each other better. You set the standards and expect each other to rise up to meet them.

If someone is not giving their maximum effort, you have a crucial conversation with them and challenge and love and encourage them through the process. If someone is facing a personal challenge, then of course you support and comfort them through it as both a family and team member. But professionally, you don't allow your team to be comfortable with the status quo. Discomfort leads to growth, so you keep raising the bar and pushing your team out of their comfort zone while pursuing excellence and growth together.

If you love someone, you don't let them settle for less than their best. You help each person reach their full potential. My wife is not afraid to call me out and she makes me better. My children make me better. I push my kids to be their best. Because I love them, I won't let them settle. Because I love them, I won't make it easy. I know that we can't just be a great family. We also have to be a great team.

Loving each other, holding each other accountable, and making each other better makes you a better family and team.

Love Tough

Two words you and your team need to remember to make sure love and accountability work well together are *love tough*. I believe in tough love but love must come first. Love must arrive before truth.

If you truly knew that someone had your best interests in mind would you be more open to hearing their feedback? Of course you would and that's your task as a team: to make sure each team member knows you have their best interest in mind. If you hit someone with constructive criticism, they are less likely to be open to hear it if they don't think you care about them. If they know you love them, they will likely be more open. If you talk about love and accountability, and love tough as a team, you can put these essential principles into practice and make them a part of your culture—and be stronger for it. The more you love, the tougher you are.

Love tough = stronger together.

Positive Discontent

Positive teams in their quest for growth and excellence have positive discontent. This means that whether they succeed or fail, they are always looking to get better. Even if they win the account or meet their deadline or win an award or the big game, great teams ask, "What can we do better? How can we improve?"

They are never satisfied because they know improvement is always possible. They also have a healthy perspective when they fail, lose, or experience a rejection. They don't get discouraged. They get better. They don't get down. They lift up and identify ways they can improve individually and collectively.

Tell-the-Truth Mondays

My friend Yogi Roth, who is a college football analyst with the Pac-12 Network, coached with Pete Carroll at University of Southern California. Pete created Tell-the-Truth Mondays. Yogi said that, after their games, the team would gather together on Monday and talk about what they did wrong, how they can improve, and what they would need to do to get better.

Yogi said it was refreshing because it was a session to simply share the truth about what happened and what needed to change. It wasn't about blaming anyone or making someone feel bad. It was about getting better as a team. It became a part of their culture and everyone expected the truth, received the truth, and saw the discussion as a growth opportunity.

Yogi said if you want to be a great team, you have to have the difficult conversations. You have to be open to and desire feedback in order to get better. You have to give each other the opportunity to speak truth and grow from the truth.

With Tell-the-Truth Mondays you have the conversation in an honest, transparent, and demanding but not demeaning way, and then everyone moves forward together to make the rest of the week great.

Have the Difficult Conversations

They're not always fun, but if you are open to having difficult conversations with your team, they lead to positive growth for everyone.

Kerri Walsh Jennings told me that having difficult conversations with her volleyball partner, Misty May-Treanor, was a huge part of winning the gold medal in London in the 2012 Olympics. While working with sports psychologist Michael Gervais, she and Misty had critical conversations filled with healthy conflict; worked out minor issues so they didn't become big issues; got to the core of who they were; became deeply connected; and performed as a united, powerful, and positive team.

Michael Gervais told me that, as a team, you must be able to communicate clearly during emotionally charged conversations and challenging circumstances. He calls these moments "storming" and you must move through the storming effectively.

The way you do this is to expect that difficult conversations are part of the process of becoming a great team and, as a team, you decide the rules of engagement. As a team you say, "This is how we do things here. This is how we handle conflict. This is how we have difficult conversations. This is how we stay calm when having an emotionally charged conversation."

Kerri brought this approach to her partnership with Misty and also to her relationship with her husband and they experienced a deeper level of intimacy, unity, and strength as a result.

I can relate to what Kerri told me because my wife and I have had difficult conversations for years, but they always made us stronger. I believe one of the reasons why we have stayed together and have relationship grit through all the challenges in our life is because we were open to feedback and were willing to get better for each other.

I remember my wife one day said, "I think you need to be a better father. Can I give you some suggestions?" At first I wanted to be defensive but instead I said, "Sure. Make me better." After hearing her advice, I committed to doing a few things and it made us a better parenting team and made our family a better team as well.

Don't run from the difficult conversation. Don't be scared of feedback. It's not meant to define you. It's meant to help refine you so you can do your job better for your team. Decide how you do things here and, when everyone knows how to engage and what to do and what to expect, you will become a stronger team.

Like versus Love

Steve Shenbaum, who works with teams using game dynamics, told me that one thing that's holding teams back from being stronger is the individual's desire to be liked. Because team members don't want people to dislike them and get upset with them, they don't share truth and don't engage in difficult conversations.

Steve said he's seen it more since the world of social media is built on *likes*. "Everyone wants to be liked, and so they just stay surface level without revealing anything that may lead to dislike. They don't want to disagree, either, because they think that will lead to dislike."

This is a really important point because some people might assume that being positive means you don't have conflict and you smile at your team members all the time. This couldn't be further from the truth.

Yogi Roth said, "Teams must understand the difference between disagreement and dislike. You have to have the difficult conversations, but you do them in a positive way." You don't just stand up and start telling everyone what's wrong with them and disagree because you are angry and upset. You do it with the intent to learn, grow, and address issues that need to be addressed. You do it to make the team better. It won't be toxic if you have a positive intention, storm effectively (as Michael Gervais suggests), and are clear about the spirit in which it is being shared.

Steve Shenbaum said it all comes down to like and love. "If you are a team that wants to just like each other, then simply communicate at the surface level. Have fun, laugh, and stay away from difficult conversations. But if you and your team just want to be liked and don't have difficult conversations, then you will never grow to love each other."

It's through the challenges, conflict, vulnerability, transparency, and connection that great teams are refined and formed. You can be satisfied with *like* or you can become a positive and powerful team that does what it takes to foster intimacy and *love*.

Forged in the Fire

Michael Gervais told me point blank, "Shared experiences are hard. No one said it was easy to build a great team. It's easy to be average. It's hard to be a great team." As you can see, it takes a lot of effort and energy to build the culture and have the conversations that make you a better team.

Gervais said, "It's easy when the vision is clear and the commitment has been made and positive results are coming back. But when things aren't going well and issues arise, that is when great teams come together. Through connected relationships they commit to their vision and purpose and take care of each other and execute together. Great teams are made when they are forged in the fire of conflict, and through confrontation they come out stronger."

Just as teammates must have certain physical, mental, and technical skills, they must also have emotional skills to grow together. It's not easy to go through this process of becoming a great team—but it's worth it.

Chapter 9

We Are Better Together

When we are part of a great team, we find a collective greatness we won't find on our own.

As I was writing this book, I received an email from Brandon Farrar, a 28-year-old teacher in Mechanicsville, Virginia. At the high school where he teaches, he formed a leadership study group consisting of 27 sophomore students and two senior leaders. He started the club knowing that these sophomores will be at the school for the next three years and it would be a great investment to positively encourage them and help guide them in leadership experiences.

The seniors serve as mentor figures and help run the club. Brandon said they meet every other week for an official meeting (about 40 minutes) during school, where they use my book, *The Positive Dog*, to guide discussions, do team-building activities, and engage in volunteer opportunities. Brandon said,

So far the guys have served lunch to our cafeteria staff, and written letters of gratitude to people that work in the building. These guys would now describe themselves as brothers. Most recently, one of our student's mother passed away, and the outpouring of love coming from these guys has been incredible. The affected student continued to say over and over again how he wanted to stay as positive as possible.

After reading Brandon's email, I realized that he and his group of young men were a team. Perhaps they aren't what one would think of as a traditional team, but nevertheless they have come together as a team for a common purpose—and in doing so they have impacted themselves, each other, their school, and their community.

People come together to form all types of teams. Some teams row a boat. Some design the boat; others build the boat. Some teams build bridges and others build bridges to the future by creating new technology and medicine. Some teams play for championships, while other teams make it possible for people to watch the championships on television. Some teams teach children in schools, while other teams create the curriculum children learn. Some teams work in an office, while others are virtual. Some teams are temporary, while others stay together for decades. Some teams come together for a season, but no matter how long people work together, I'm convinced they come together for a reason. We come together because we are better together.

Ryan Coogler, director of the blockbuster movie *Black Panther*, in a letter of appreciation to the public wrote that "Filmmaking is a team sport. And our team was made up of amazing people from all over the world who believed in this story."

Peter Smith, the coach of USC tennis, told me that on his first call with every recruit he says, "If you come here, you are coming here to be part of a team. Tennis is an individual sport, but you are coming here to be part of a team." The young men usually hear this and probably don't give it much thought but, over time, they learn that when people commit to something bigger than themselves, they rise to a level much higher than themselves.

Donna Orender founded Generation W as a way to unite and connect women. She found that, individually, a woman can accomplish a lot by using her talent and ambition and will. But by becoming a part of a larger team of women, they can go far above and beyond what they could do alone. Talent will only take someone so far, but with a team they can create the impossible.

Kerri Walsh Jennings added that love does not come from winning. Winning comes from love. Love comes when you fight for it. The game and the goals are simply ways for us to unite, commit, lean in, fight, and grow *together* and for each other. In the process, we discover that greatness is never achieved in isolation. We are better together, and when we are together we get better individually.

Tom Brady isn't the greatest quarterback without Bill Belichick, and Bill Belichick isn't the greatest coach without Tom Brady. They became the greatest together. Kerri Walsh Jennings and Misty May-Treanor aren't the greatest beach volleyball team of all time on their own. Steve Jobs wouldn't have been Steve Jobs without Steve Wozniak, and vice versa. Jodi Foster and Anthony Hopkins made each other great in *The Silence of the Lambs*. John Lennon and Paul McCartney made the Beatles (and Ringo) great. The megahit television series *The Bible* would have never been made if Roma Downey and Mark Burnett had never met in a hair salon and, subsequently, fallen in love. While, individually, she acted in and he produced great shows prior to *The Bible*, they found an uncommon greatness and co-produced a Hollywood miracle together. Speaking of Hollywood, Steven Spielberg, George Lucas, Martin Scorsese, Brian de Palma, and Francis Ford Coppola spent a lot of time together as young filmmakers where they challenged each other, consulted with one another, and made revolutionary movies that transformed the movie industry forever. Without their friendships and teamwork we may never have had iconic movies such as *Star Wars*, *ET*, and *Indiana Jones*.

And in my own small world, I wouldn't be me without my wife and the love of my life, Kathryn. She stood by me and believed in me through all our challenges and ups and downs. She put up with me when I was very negative. She helped me work through my past issues and become a better man and leader. She took care of our children when I was on the road speaking a lot. She encouraged me to go after my dream as a writer. She gave me strength and encouragement when I wanted to give up. She gave me love and support so that I could give love and support to others. Without her, I wouldn't be the man I am today.

I also couldn't have written this book without my publishing team of Shannon Vargo and Matt Holt. They took a chance on me 12 years ago and, without them, *The Energy Bus* and my other books may have never been published. I've been offered a lot more money to go to other publishers, but why would I leave a team that believed in me when others didn't? Why would I abandon people who are committed to me and have become my family? I believe in the team we have become. I know that when we are part of a great team, together we find a collective greatness we won't find on our own.

I have found there comes a moment when a team becomes a real team. You can look back at your marriage, sports team, work team, school team, community team, creative team and say YES, that's when we really came together. It's hard to describe, but it's a special feeling when it happens.

For the Clemson university basketball team, it was a terrorist attack that helped bring them together as a team this year. Last season they talked a lot about grit but they weren't very gritty. They lost a lot of close games because they weren't connected as a team. But this year they had their best season in years and one of the reasons is, while playing in Europe, a terrorist attack happened outside their hotel. Several of their players weren't accounted for and for a brief time they expected the worst. When all the players were finally accounted for they had a newfound appreciation for life and for what they meant to each other. A bond was formed that has translated to more connection, commitment, and grit on the court.

Brian Kopplemen had known David Levien since they were 16 and 14 years old but, when they were deep into writing the movie *Rounders*, they truly became a team. For them, being a team meant that when they decided to work on a project together, they wouldn't let anyone or anything get in the way of that.

Maura Neville, a principal at one of our Energy Bus schools said she realized her staff had become a team when, during her second year, people were coming together more and more for the sake of each other and their students. She said, "I watched teams of teachers reflect on their practices and start doing things for the kids and not so much for themselves. I noticed teachers investing in the relationships they were building and truly connecting on a family level.

We Are Better Together

When I started here the staff was more centered on serving themselves rather than others, but I watched them transform before my eyes and serve each other. That's when I knew we had become a team."

Steve Strickland, the general manager of a Lexus store for Hendrick Automotive, told me he realized his staff had become a team when one of his top sales guys had to take a leave of absence to take care of his sick mother and everyone rallied together to meet their team goals and objectives. He said it's not the win that makes you a team. It's the way you rally and come together to create the win.

My hope for you and your team is that you will experience the power of the moment I'm describing, where you and your team know you have become a positive, united team. My hope is that reading this book together will help you experience and demonstrate the power of a positive team.

It won't happen overnight. Anything worthwhile and meaningful takes time to build. But if you implement the framework and principles we discussed in this book, you will do far more together than you can accomplish on your own.

We are better together and, together as a positive team, you will do amazing things. The best is yet to come to those who believe and work together to make it so. Are you ready? Gather your team and get started! It's time to leave your legacy.

Meraki

Meraki is one of my favorite words. It's a Greek word that means to do something with love, soul, and creativity; to leave a piece of yourself in your work; to leave something behind.

As a team you can leave a piece of yourselves in your work, and together you can leave a legacy. You can be the team that does what has never been done before. You can be the team that begins a winning tradition that is enjoyed by everyone who comes after you. You can be the team that invents the new product or technology that changes the world. You can be the team that creates a new blockbuster movie. You can be the team that transforms healthcare or education. You can be the team that changes everything.

The 2017 University of Maryland lacrosse team will always be remembered as a national champion. But more importantly they will be remembered as a team that stayed positive, committed, cared, and played for others more than themselves.

When my friend and former teammate, John Tillman, became the head coach of Maryland lacrosse in 2011, all he heard was that Maryland hadn't won a national championship since 1975. Over the ensuing years, under John's leadership, the team made it to the national championship game in 2011, 2012, 2015, and 2016, but lost each time.

In 2017 the cries continued that Maryland hadn't won a championship in 42 years. As the team marched toward another national championship game, there was both excitement and fear from the fan base that this would be the year they win it all or lose another one.

You could imagine there would be a lot of pressure on the team to win, but John told me that the team really didn't feel a lot of pressure because they didn't want to win a championship for themselves. They wanted to win for all the fans and all the past players who came close but didn't win. The team wanted to win for John, whose mother had passed away before the season. They wanted to win for their honorary team member, Fionn, a boy who was battling cancer and became an inspirational member of the team. They wanted to win for their university.

They were committed to playing for something greater than themselves. They cared about *we* more than *me*. Instead of focusing on themselves and feeling pressure, they focused on playing for others and felt inspiration, passion, and purpose. It's a great lesson for all teams.

When you become a positive team and make it about *we* instead of *me*, you become the team you know you can be. You don't have to be pessimistic; you can be optimistic. You don't have to be selfish; you can be selfless. You don't have to be average; you can be special. You can be the team that shows the world what a great team that believes, unites, commits, and cares looks like. You can leave something behind that makes things better for the people that follow you. Great teams leave a legacy and you can start creating yours today!

Are You a Real Team?

Many people think that just because they are *on* a team, they are part of a real team. That isn't the case. Being on a team doesn't make you a team. Being a *real* team is what makes a group of people into a team. Consider the following:

- People who are just on a team focus on their own goals.
- People who are part of a real team focus on team goals first and their individual goals second.

- Individuals just on a team are committed to getting better and improving themselves.
- Individuals who are part of a real team are not only committed to self-improvement, but they are also committed to making each other and the team better.

- People just on a team think about how the team can serve their desires.
- People who are part of a real team desire to serve the team.

- When people are just on a team, communication isn't a priority.
- When people are a real team, communication is essential to build trust, commitment, and teamwork.

- On a team, each individual's time is more important than the team.
- A real team member makes time with the team a priority.

- On a team, trust, love, and respect are not often discussed or cultivated.
- A real team focuses on building trust, sharing love, and showing respect.

- On a team, people fight, which hurts the team because members don't have trust and love.
- On a real team, members also fight, but the fighting makes the team stronger because they have trust and love. They grow from their disagreements.

- On a team, not everyone is on the bus.
- On a real team, everyone is on the bus and with a shared vision, focus, and purpose.

- On a team, there's a lack of leadership.
- On a real team, there are strong leaders who develop other leaders.

- People just on a team have egos and want to be great.
- People who are part of a real team also have egos and want to be great, but they give up their egos to serve their team and a bigger cause in order to be truly great.

Are You a Real Team?

11 Thoughts about Teamwork

1. **Teams rise and fall on culture, leadership, relationships, attitude, and effort.**

   Great teams have a great culture driven by great leadership. Relationships are meaningful and teammates are connected. The collective attitude is very positive and everyone on the team works hard to accomplish their shared mission.

2. **It's all about teamwork. Sometimes you are the star and sometimes you help the star.**

3. **If want to be truly great, you have to work as hard to be a great teammate as you do to be a great player.**

   I tell this to athletes all the time, but the same is true for any profession. When we work hard to be great team members, we make everyone around us better.

4. **Your team doesn't care if you are a superstar. They care if you are a super team member.**

5. **Three things you control every day are your attitude, your effort, and your actions to be a great teammate.**

   It doesn't matter what is happening around you and who you think is being unfair. Every day you can focus on being positive, working hard, and making others around you better. If you do that, great things will happen.

6. **One person can't make a team but one person can break a team. Stay positive!**

Make sure you don't let energy vampires sabotage your team. Post a sign that says "No energy vampires allowed" and keep them off the bus. Most importantly, decide to stay positive.

7. **Great team members hold each other accountable to the high standards and excellence their culture expects and demands.**

8. **Team beats talent when talent isn't a team.**

9. **Great teams care more. They care more about their effort, their work, and their teammates.**

10. **We > me.**

    Unity is the difference between a great team and an average team. United teams are connected and committed to each other. They are selfless instead of selfish. They put the team first and know that together they accomplish more.

11. **You and your team face a fork in the road each day. You can settle for average and choose the path of mediocrity, or you can take the road less traveled and chase greatness.**

    It's a choice you make each day. Which path will your team take?

    Download this as a poster at www.PowerofaPositiveTeam.com

11 Thoughts about Teamwork

References

Baker, W., Cross, R., and Wooten, M. (2003). Positive organizational network analysis and energizing relationships. In: *Positive Organizational Scholarship: Foundations of a New Discipline* (ed. J. Cameron, J.E. Dutton, and R. Quinn), 328–342. San Francisco, CA: Berrett-Koehler.

Boyatzis, R., Rochford, K., and Taylor, S. (2015). *The Impact of Shared Vision on Leadership, Engagement, and Organizational Citizenship*. Lausanne, Switzerland: Frontiers Media.

Cerretani, J. (2018). The contagion of happiness. Harvard Medical School. https://hms.harvard.edu/news/harvard-medicine/contagion-happiness.

Croft, A., Dunn, E., and Quoidbach, J. (2014). From tribulations to appreciation: experiencing adversity in the past predicts greater savoring in the present. *Social Psychological and Personality Science*, 5 (5): 511–516.

Duckworth, A., and Peterson, C. (2007). Grit: perseverance and passion for long-term goals. *Journal of Personality and Social Psychology*, 92 (6): 1087–1101.

Fredrickson, B. (2001). The role of positive emotions in positive psychology: the broaden-and-build theory of positive emotions. *American Psychologist*, 56: 218–226.

Gottman, J. (1994). *Why Marriages Succeed or Fail*. New York: Simon & Schuster.

LeClerc, M. (2017). The effect of gratitude on cortisol reactivity. *Manoa Horizons*, 2: 106–116.

McCraty, R., Atkinson, M., Tomasino, D., and Tiller, W. (1998). The electricity of touch: detection and measurement of cardiac energy exchange between people. In: *Brain Values: Is a Biological Science of Values Possible* (ed. K.H. Pribram), 359–379. Mahway, NJ: Lawrence Erlbaum.

Puro, M., and Robinson, D. T. (2007). Optimism and Economic Choice. *Journal of Financial Economics*, 86:71–79.

Rath, T. (2007). *Strengths Finder 2.0*. New York: Gallup.

Reptilian coping brain. (2017). http://www.copingskills4kids. net/Reptilian_Coping_Brain.html.

Let us help you build a Positive, United, and Connected Team

KEYNOTE

VIDEO PROGRAM

ACTION PLAN

OFFSITE TEAM-BUILDING

Visit www.PowerOfAPositiveTeam.com
or call 904-285-6842 for more information.

Power of a Positive Team
Resources

Visit www.PowerOfAPositiveTeam.com for:

- Action Plans
- Posters
- Video Program
- Training

If you are interested in contacting Jon Gordon and his team, please contact The Jon Gordon Companies at:

Phone: 904-285-6842

E-email: info@jongordon.com

Online: JonGordon.com

Twitter: @JonGordon11

Facebook: Facebook.com/JonGordonpage

Instagram: JonGordon11

Sign up for Jon's weekly positive tip at: JonGordon.com.

Positive Inspiration,
Encouragement and Lessons
that will help you overcome your challenges and make a greater impact.

Positive University (Positive U) is a free online resource designed to equip people with positive inspiration, encouragement, and lessons that will help them overcome their challenges and make a greater impact.

It's 100 Percent FREE and includes access to videos and podcasts from bestselling author Jon Gordon and his guests.

Guests have included: Coach Dabo Swinney from Clemson University, Bestselling Author Ken Blanchard, Pastor Erwin McManus, LA Rams Coach Sean McVay, Bestselling Author Ryan Holiday, NY Giants Wide Receiver Brandon Marshall, Movie Producer DeVon Franklin, and many more.

—— *Go to* ——
PositiveUniversity.co

Other Books by Jon Gordon

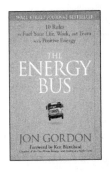

Energy Bus

A man whose life and career are in shambles learns from a unique bus driver and set of passengers how to overcome adversity. Enjoy an enlightening ride of positive energy that is improving the way leaders lead, employees work, and teams function. www.TheEnergyBus.com

No Complaining Rule

Follow a VP of Human Resources who must save herself and her company from ruin, and discover proven principles and an actionable plan to win the battle against individual and organizational negativity. www.NoComplainingRule.com

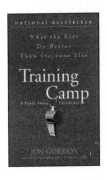

Training Camp

This inspirational story about a small guy with a big heart and a special coach who guides him on a quest for excellence reveals the eleven winning habits that separate the best individuals and teams from the rest. www.TrainingCamp11.com

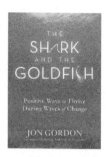

The Shark and the Goldfish

Delightfully illustrated, this quick read is packed with tips and strategies on how to respond to challenges beyond your control in order to thrive during the waves of change.

www.SharkandGoldfish.com

Soup

The newly anointed CEO of a popular soup company is brought in to reinvigorate the brand and bring success back to a company that has fallen on hard times. Through her journey, discover the key ingredients to unite, engage, and inspire teams and create a culture of greatness.

www.Soup11.com

The Seed

Go on a quest for the meaning and passion behind work with Josh, an up-and-comer at his company who is disenchanted with his job. Through Josh's cross-country journey, you'll find surprising new sources of wisdom and inspiration in your own business and life.

www.Seed11.com

Other Books by Jon Gordon

The Positive Dog

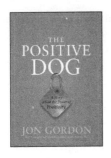

We all have two dogs inside of us. One dog is positive, happy, optimistic, and hopeful. The other dog is negative, mad, pessimistic, and fearful. These two dogs often fight inside us, but guess who wins the fight? The one you feed the most. *The Positive Dog* is an inspiring story that not only reveals the strategies and benefits of being positive but also an essential truth for humans: Being positive doesn't just make you better. It makes everyone around you better.

www.feedthepositivedog.com

One Word

One Word is a simple concept that delivers powerful life change! This quick read will inspire you to simplify your life and work by focusing on just one word for this year. *One Word* creates clarity, power, passion, and life-change. When you find your word, live it, and share it, your life will become more rewarding and exciting than ever.

www.getoneword.com

The Carpenter

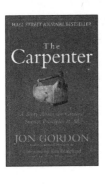

The Carpenter is Jon Gordon's most inspiring book yet—filled with powerful lessons and the greatest success strategies of all. Michael wakes up in the hospital with a bandage on his head and fear in his heart, after collapsing while on a morning jog. When Michael finds out the man who saved his life is a Carpenter, he visits him and quickly learns that he is more than just a Carpenter; he is also a builder of lives, careers, people, and teams. In this journey, you will learn the timeless principles to help you stand out, excel, and make an impact on people and the world.

www.carpenter11.com

The Hard Hat

A true story about Cornell lacrosse player George Boiardi, *The Hard Hat* is an unforgettable book about a selfless, loyal, joyful, hard-working, competitive, and compassionate leader and teammate; the impact he had on his team and program; and the lessons we can learn from him. This inspirational story will help you discover how to be the best teammate you can be and how to build a great team.

www.hardhat21.com

You Win in the Locker Room First: The 7 C's to Build a Winning Team in Business, Sports, and Life

Based on the extraordinary experiences of NFL Coach Mike Smith and leadership expert Jon Gordon, *You Win in the Locker Room First* offers a rare, behind-the-scenes look at one of the most pressure-packed leadership jobs on the planet and what leaders can learn from these experiences in order to build their own winning team.

www.wininthelockerroom.com

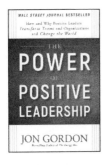

The Power of Positive Leadership

The Power of Positive Leadership is your personal coach for becoming the leader your people deserve. Storyteller Jon Gordon gathers the insights from all of his best-selling fables to bring you the definitive guide to positive leadership. Difficult times call for leaders who are up for the challenge. Results are the by-product of your culture, teamwork, vision, talent, innovation, execution, and commitment. This book shows you how to bring it all together to become a powerfully positive leader.

www.powerofpositiveleadership.com

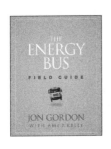

The Energy Bus Field Guide

The Energy Bus Field Guide is your roadmap to fueling your life, work, and team with positive energy. The international bestseller, *The Energy Bus*, has helped millions of people from around the world shift to a more positive outlook; the story of George and Joy bus driver has resonated with people from all walks of life, each with their own individual vision of "success." This guide is designed as a practical companion to help you *live and share* the ten principles every day, with real, actionable steps you can immediately put into practice in your life, work, team, and organization.

Other Books by Jon Gordon

Life Word

Life Word reveals a simple, powerful tool to help you identify the word that will inspire you to live your best life while leaving your greatest legacy. In the process you'll discover your *why*, which will help show you the way to live with a renewed sense of power, purpose, and passion. www.getoneword.com/lifeword

Thank You and Good Night

Thank You and Good Night is a beautifully illustrated book that shares the heart of gratitude. Jon Gordon takes a little boy and girl on a fun-filled journey from one perfect moonlit night to the next. During their adventurous days and nights, the children explore the people, places, and things that they are thankful for.

The two tots in *Thank You and Good Night* learn that being thankful makes ice cream taste better, butterflies look more beautiful, and weekend days seem longer. "Thank you" is a phrase that will brighten any kid's day and help them get a good night's sleep.

The Hard Hat for Kids

The Hard Hat for Kids is an illustrated guide to teamwork. Adapted from the bestseller *The Hard Hat*, this book presents the same inspirational message and motivational tone in a way that resonates with children who have ever played a team sport, belonged to a club, or worked on a group project for school.

This uplifting story presents practical insights and life-changing lessons that are immediately applicable to everyday situations, giving kids—and adults—a new outlook on cooperation and communication.

Mickey is a spunky basketball lover who has always dreamed about playing on her school's team. On the first day of practice, she learns of a special award given to the best teammate—and soon learns that there is a big difference between being the best player and being the best teammate. What follows is an unforgettable story about selflessness, loyalty, hard work, and compassion, and a clear lesson on putting the team first.

The Energy Bus for Kids

The illustrated children's adaptation of the bestselling book *The Energy Bus* tells the story of George, who, with the help of his school bus driver, Joy, learns that if he believes in himself, he'll find the strength to overcome any challenge. His journey teaches kids how to overcome negativity, bullies, and everyday challenges to be their best.

www.EnergyBusKids.com